Learn to Cook

Healthy Wok
& Stir-fry Dishes

Stir-fried dishes are the ultimate in
Asian "comfort food." Included here
are over 65 quick and delicious recipes
prepared with a wok.

PERIPLUS

Contents

Introduction	3
Ingredients	4
Vegetable Dishes	8
Tofu and *Tempe* Dishes	40
Stir-fried Noodles	46
Rice Dishes	60
Fish and Seafood Dishes	72
Chicken Dishes	98
Meat Dishes	111
Complete Recipe Listing	128

MAIL ORDER SOURCES

Finding the ingredients for Asian home cooking has become very simple. Most supermarkets carry staples such as soy sauce, fresh ginger, and fresh lemongrass. Almost every large metropolitan area has Asian markets serving the local population—just check your local business directory. With the Internet, exotic Asian ingredients and cooking utensils can be easily found online. The following list is a good starting point of online merchants offering a wide variety of goods and services.

http://www.asiafoods.com
http://www.geocities.com/MadisonAvenue/8074/VarorE.html
http://dmoz.org/Shopping/Food/Ethnic_and_Regional/Asian/
http://templeofthai.com/
http://www.orientalpantry.com/
http://www.zestyfoods.com/
http://www.thaigrocer.com/Merchant/index.htm
http://asianwok.com/
http://pilipinomart.com/
http://www.indiangrocerynet.com/
http://www.orientalfoodexpress.com/

Mention "wok and stir-fry," and one immediately visualizes a huge heaving wok being wielded above a mighty flame by an Asian chef. One also thinks Asian "comfort food" — with accompanying images of nurturing, wholesome, and thoughtfully prepared meals, meant to be eaten together with family members in the comfort of the home.

While here there is sometimes still a mystique that Asian chefs meticulously prepare all their ingredients in the elaborate ancestral manner, the truth is many home chefs — here, as in Asia — can now hardly afford the time to do so. Hence stir-frying is one of the best cooking methods for modern cooks and families — because of the intense heat required, the food is cooked rapidly, and its taste and nutritional value are well preserved. And the Chinese wok is the most essential implement in stir-frying, as its deep, bowl-like shape and sloping sides ensures that the ingredients remain in the center, where the heat is most intense.

The aim of *Healthy Wok and Stir-fry Dishes* is to introduce nutritious and easy-to-prepare Asian stir-fry favorites, ranging from the ubiquitous Chinese Cabbage and Tofu Skin Stir-fried with Ginger, Hot and Spicy Tofu, and Stir-fried Sliced Fish with Ginger, to the classic *Gung Bao* Squid with Dried Chilies, Classic Thai Fried Rice, and Five-spice Chicken with Garlic and Scallions.

All of the recipes in this volume are light, healthy, and tasty, requiring no special skills or ingredients to prepare. May this book bring endless cooking pleasure and gastronomic joy as you venture into the world of Asian cuisine.

Ingredients

Asian basil has pointed dark green leaves and a strong anise aroma and taste. Fresh basil leaves are used to garnish dishes. Substitute fresh Italian basil.

Asian eggplants are long and slender, smaller and slightly sweeter than the commonplace Western variety. Asian eggplants are either purple or green.

Bean thread noodles are also known as "cellophane" or "glass" noodles, and are thin, clear strands made from mung bean starch and water. Soak in hot water for 15 minutes to soften. Available from Asian food stores.

Cayenne pepper is a pungent red powder made from ground chili peppers, also known as ground red pepper. Substitute dried red chili flakes or chili paste.

Chili oil is made from dried chilies or chili powder steeped in oil, which is used to enliven some Sichuan dishes.

Chili paste consists of pounded chilies, sometimes mixed with vinegar, sold in jars. The heat varies from brand to brand. Sichuan chili paste is made from dried chilies, soaked and ground with a touch of oil.

Chinese peashoots (*dou miao*) are the delicate leaves at the top of pea plants. They are particularly good when stir-fried simply with a little oil and garlic. Substitute spinach or any other leafy green.

Coriander leaves, also known as cilantro, are widely used as a flavoring and garnish. Fresh coriander leaves have a strong taste and aroma and can be refrigerated in a plastic bag for about one week. Parsley is a suitable substitute. **Coriander seeds** are used as a spice in Asian curries.

Crispy fried shallots are a popular garnish for many Asian dishes, and are readily available at Asian food stores. They are also easily prepared (see recipe on page 7).

Curry leaves comprise sprigs of small, dark green leaves wit a distinctive fragrance. They are often used in Indian dishes to add aroma and flavor. Fresh curry leaves should be used within a few days of purchase. Dried curry leaves keep well if stored in a dry place. Substitute bay leaves.

Fish sauce is a fermented fish product generally made by layering fish and salt in large jars and then siphoning off the liquid. It is a common seasoning in Thai and Vietnamese food.

Five-spice powder is a Chinese ground spice combination of star anise, Sichuan peppercorns, fennel, cloves, and cinnamon. It is used in meat marinades and soup stocks. This mixture is very strong, and should be used in small amounts.

Garam masala is an Indian blend of several strongly aromatic spices designed to add flavor and fragrance to meat dishes. Powdered *garam masala* is available from stores specializing in spices.

Kaffir lime leaves are the fragrant leaves of the kaffir lime plant. The leaves are used whole in soups and curries, or shredded finely and added to salads.

Lentils are protein- and fiber-rich legumes often referred to in Asia by their Indian name, *dal*. Two kinds of lentils are used in this book. **Split chickpeas** or *garbanzos* (*channa dal*) resemble yellow split peas, which may be used as a substitute. **Black lentils** (*urad dal*) are sold either with their black skin on or husked, when they are creamy white in color.

Lotus root is the thick root of the aquatic lotus plant and is available fresh in many Chinese grocery stores. It is either covered in mud or cleaned and scaled and wrapped in plastic. A good substitute is *jicama* (yam bean) or cauliflower.

Mushrooms are prized in Asian cooking for the flavor and texture they add to dishes. *Shiitake* or Chinese black mushrooms are generally large and meaty, and are used in soups, stir-fries, and side dishes, or as a meat substitute. Research has shown that *shiitake* mushrooms boost the human immune system. Fresh *shiitake* are increasingly available in supermarkets. Substitute dried mushrooms or *porcini* mushrooms. If using dried mushrooms, soak in hot water for 10 to 15 minutes to soften, then drain. Remove the stems and discard. **Wood ear mushrooms**, also known as cloud ear fungus, are available dried, and have a crunchy texture and a delicate woodsy flavor. They must also be soaked in hot water beforehand.

Oyster sauce is a flavorsome soy-based sauce with oyster extract: a Cantonese speciality. The vegetarian version is available, and sometimes sold as "mushroom oyster sauce."

Palm sugar is made from the refined sap of the sugar palm. Available in Asian grocery stores, it is usually sold in small disks that are $1/_2$-in (1-cm) thick and 3-in ($7^1/_2$-cm) wide, or are sometimes sold in larger cellophane-wrapped blocks. Substitute dark brown sugar or maple syrup.

Rice wine or *sake* adds a sweet, subtle flavor to dishes. It is used in Chinese cooking as a tenderizer, to blend flavors and enhance taste. It is widely available in Asian grocery stores and the specialty food section of some supermarkets. Dry sherry is a good substitute.

Shrimp paste is sold under its Malay name, *belacan*, and available dried and wet. Shrimp paste should be roasted before use: either wrap in foil and roast, dry-ry in a pan, or roast over a gas flame on the back of a spoon. Dried shrimp paste is usually sold as a crumbly pink to brown block.

Shrimp paste dip is also known by its Malay name, *sambal balacan*. (See recipe on page 7). Shrimp paste dip is served as an accompaniment to main dishes such as Black Hokkien Noodles (page 56).

Sichuan pepper, also known as flower pepper or fagara, has a sharp pungence that tingles and slightly numbs the lips and tongue, an effect known in Chinese as *ma la* ("numb hot"). Sprinkle over cooked dishes as garnish. (See recipe on page 7).

Soy sauce is probably the best known Asian seasoning agent, made from fermented soya beans. Three varieties are used in this book: **thin**, or the common Chinese soy sauce, which is lighter in color and saltier than **thick** soy sauce, which is a dark but milder version; and **sweet** soy sauce, which is very dark and sweetish. The latter is frequently used as a condiment as well as a seasoning; substitute thick black Chinese soy sauce and sweeten with brown sugar.

Soybean paste is made from made from fermented black or yellow soybeans, and is an important seasoning in Asian dishes. **Black bean paste** has a strong, salty flavor, while **yellow soybean paste** is slightly sweet. Soybean pastes are available at Asian food stores. After use, the paste should be stored in a tightly sealed container in the refrigerator.

Star anise is a dark brown, strongly-flavored spice that resembles an eight-pointed star. Its aroma is similar to anise or cinnamon. Store in a tightly-sealed jar in a cool, dry place.

Tamarind juice is commonly available in the form of pulp which must soaked in water, stirred, squeezed, and strained to yield a sourish liquid that adds a subtle citrus flavor to a dish. (See recipe on page 7).

Tempe is a compressed, lightly fermented soybean cake with a nutty flavor. Often available in Asian food stores. No substitute.

Tofu (bean curd) is available firm or soft. **Firm tofu** stays in shape when cut or cooked and has a stronger, slightly sour taste. **Soft tofu** is slippery and tends to crumble easily but has a more silky texture and refined flavor. **Tofu skin** is the thin rich layer of soy protein that forms on the surface of soy bean milk while it is being boiled to make tofu. The dried variety, or **tofu sheet**, is available in most Asian grocery stores. It has the same nutritional benefits and is easier to work with in the kitchen, although it is less tasty than tofu skin. Tofu sheet is commonly used in stir-fries and vegetarian cooking as a meat substitute.

Water spinach is also known as water convolvulus and by its Malay name, *kangkung*. This aquatic plant is rich in protein and minerals such as iron.

White fungus is also known as dried white wood ears. It is a crinkly golden dried fungus that becomes transparent after soaking. It adds a crunchy texture to dishes and is often used in Chinese soups and desserts.

Crispy Fried Shallots

6 to 8 shallots, peeled and thinly sliced
1/4 cup (125ml) oil

Heat oil in a frying pan or wok over medium heat and fry the sliced shallots until golden brown, taking great care not to over-brown them as this makes them taste bitter. Carefully remove fried shallots with a slotted spoon, transferring them onto a plate lined with paper toweling. If not using immediately, store in a dry, airtight jar to preserve their crispiness.

Shrimp Paste Dip (Sambal Belacan)

3 red chililes, chopped
3 teaspoons crumbled roasted shrimp paste (belacan)
1 teaspoon sugar
1/4 teaspoon salt
1 tablespoon lime juice

Slice the chilies and pound finely in a mortar and pestle with the shrimp paste. Add the sugar, salt, and lime juice, mixing well with the pestle.

Sichuan Pepper-Salt Powder

2 tablespoons Sichuan peppercorns
1/2 teaspoon salt

Dry-toast Sichuan peppercorns with salt, then grind to a fine powder.

Tamarind Juice

3 tablespoons tamarind paste
1 cup (250 ml) water

Soak tamarind paste in the water to yield 1 cup (250 ml) tamarind juice. After soaking, discard the pulp and seeds and use the liquid.

Carrots and Shiitake Mushrooms Stir-fried with Ginger

Shiitake mushrooms have been a mainstay of Chinese cuisine for many centuries. Research has proven what Chinese cooks and herbalists have known since ancient times — that *shiitake* mushrooms give a powerful boost to the human immune system. The carrot, when combined with *shiitake*, provides a crunchy counterpoint to the chewy texture of the mushrooms and contributes its own considerable nutritional value to this dish. For some extra color and variety, try adding half a cup of fresh or frozen green peas along with the carrots.

10 to 12 dried or fresh *shiitake* mushrooms
2 carrots, washed and grated or julienned
2 tablespoons oil
1 in (2$^1/_2$ cm) fresh ginger, julienned
4 to 5 cloves garlic, minced
2 scallions, minced

Sauce
2 tablespoons rice wine
2 tablespoons soy sauce
1 teaspoon sesame oil
1 teaspoon sugar
$^1/_2$ teaspoon salt

1 If using dried mushrooms, soak in hot water for 15 minutes, then drain, reserving the liquid. Remove the stems, then slice the tops very thinly.
2 Mix together all the Sauce ingredients and set aside.
3 Heat oil in a wok over medium, then add the mushrooms, ginger, and garlic together. Stir-fry for 2 minutes, then add the sauce and continue to stir-fry for 1 minute more.
4 Add the carrots and $^1/_3$ cup (80 ml) of the mushroom water. Stir to blend, cover wok with lid, reduce heat to low, and cook for 3 to 4 minutes. Remove from heat, stir in the scallions, transfer to a platter and serve.

Serves 4
Preparation time: **20 mins**
Cooking time: **10 mins**

Carrots Stir-fried with Coconut and Curry Spices

2 tablespoons oil
1 teaspoon black lentils
1 teaspoon mustard
  seeds
1 teaspoon fennel seeds
1 dried chili, cut into
  thirds
1 onion, thinly sliced
1 green chili, seeds
  removed and sliced
2 sprigs curry leaves
1 lb (450 g) carrots,
  cubed
$1/2$ teaspoon ground
  turmeric
1 teaspoon ground
  cumin
$1/2$ teaspoon ground
  red pepper or cayenne
  pepper
$1 1/4$ teaspoons salt
1 teaspoon sugar
$1/2$ cup (125 ml) water
$1/2$ cup (50 g) fresh
  coconut, grated

1 Heat the oil in a wok over high heat and stir-fry the black lentils until golden. Add the mustard seeds, fennel seeds, and dried chilies, and stir-fry until the mustard seeds splutter and the dried chilies turn brown.
2 Add the onion, green chilies, and curry leaves. Stir-fry until the onion turns golden brown, then add the diced carrots, ground spices, salt, sugar, and water.
3 Cook, covered, until the carrots are tender and the moisture has evaporated, stirring occasionally.
4 Add the grated coconut and mix well. Stir-fry over high heat for about 2 minutes and serve.

Serves 4–6
Preparation time: **20 mins**
Cooking time: **20 mins**

Spinach Stir-fried with Garlic

3/4 lb (350 g) fresh
   spinach, stemmed, or
   Chinese peashoots
   (*dou miao*)
2 tablespoons oil
1/2 teaspoon salt
6 to 8 cloves garlic,
   sliced

Serves 4
Preparation time: **10 mins**
Cooking time: **2 mins**

1 Wash and rinse the spinach well, then place in a colander to drain.
2 Heat oil in a wok over high heat and add the salt.
3 Add the sliced garlic and the spinach, and turn carefully with a spatula to coat all the leaves with oil. Stir-fry for about 1 minute, or until all the leaves are wilted and have turned dark green. Transfer immediately to serving dish.

Chinese mustard greens or broccoli rabe are also ideal for this dish. Make sure that the vegetables are young and tender; trim the ends of the stems, and cut into bite-sized pieces.

Broccoli Stir-fried with Ginger and Onion

1½ lb (675 g) fresh
broccoli
3 tablespoons oil
6 slices fresh ginger,
minced
1 onion, cut into
crescents
1 tablespoon rice wine
mixed with 1 teaspoon
water
½ teaspoon salt

Serves 4
Preparation time: **15 mins**
Cooking time: **5 mins**

1 Cut the broccoli florets from the main stem, so that each floret retains its own stalk. Peel the tough skin from the stalks below the florets. Cut the stalks into bite-sized pieces.

2 Heat the oil in a wok over medium heat and when hot, stir in the broccoli and ginger and stir-fry about 1 minute, or until all the broccoli has turned darker green. Add the onions and cook 1 more minute.

3 Add the rice wine and water and cover tightly with a lid, steaming the broccoli for 1 to 2 minutes.

4 Removes lid, add salt, and stir to blend, then transfer to a serving dish.

Water Spinach Stir-fried with Fermented Black Beans

2 tablespoons oil
3 cloves garlic, minced
1 tablespoon fermented black bean paste
1 lb (450 g) fresh water spinach, tough stems discarded, carefully washed and snipped into 4 or 5 sections
1 red chili, sliced

1 Heat oil in a wok over high heat until very hot, and stir-fry the garlic and black bean paste, about 30 seconds.
2 Add water spinach and red chili, reduce the heat to medium, and stir-fry continuously for about 3 minutes, or until wilted and the bean paste is evenly distributed. Remove from the heat and serve.

Serves 4
Preparation time: **8 mins**
Cooking time: **10 mins**

Stir-fried Mustard Leaves and Lentils

$^1/_2$ cup (100 g)
  split chickpeas,
  washed and drained
3 cloves garlic, minced
1 teaspoon ground
  turmeric
$^1/_4$ teaspoon salt
4 cups (1 liter) water
2 tablespoons oil
1 teaspoon black lentils
1 teaspoon mustard
  seeds
1 teaspoon cumin seeds
1 dried chili, seeds
  removed and cut into
  $^1/_2$-in (1-cm) slices
1 small onion, thinly
  sliced
13 oz (400 g) mustard
  greens, cut into
  $^1/_2$-in (1-cm) pieces,
  including stalks
1 teaspoon salt
4 tablespoons grated
  fresh coconut

1 Place the split chickpeas, garlic, turmeric, salt, and water in a pan. Bring to the boil over medium heat and cook until the chickpeas are firm but slightly soft, about 20 minutes. Drain the chickpeas, reserving 5 tablespoons of the water.

2 Heat oil in a wok over high heat and stir-fry the black lentils, mustard seeds, cumin seeds, and dried chilies until the black lentils turn golden brown.

3 Add in the cooked chickpeas, mustard greens, salt, reserved chickpeas water, and grated coconut. Stir-fry until the mustard leaves are cooked

Serves 4–6
Preparation time: **15 mins**
Cooking time: **15 mins**

Chinese Cabbage and Tofu Skin Stir-fried with Ginger

1 sheet dried tofu skin (about 3 oz or 80 g), soaked in water for 10 minutes, then drained
12 oz (330 g) Chinese cabbage
1 tablespoon sesame oil
2 tablespoons oil
4 slices fresh ginger, julienned

Sauce
1 tablespoon soy sauce
1 teaspoon vinegar
1 teaspoon rice wine
1 teaspoon sugar
1 teaspoon salt

Serves 4
Preparation time: **15 mins**
Cooking time: **10 mins**

1 Cut the tofu skin into 1 x 2-in ($2^1/_2$ x 5-cm) strips. Cut the cabbage leaves to similar size.
2 Combine all the Sauce ingredients and set aside.
3 Heat oil in wok until hot but not smoking.
4 Add the tofu skin and stir-fry for 1 minute. Add the cabbage and ginger, and continue to stir-fry until the cabbage is tender, about 3 to 4 minutes.
5 Add the Sauce mixture, reduce the heat to low, and cook for 1 to 2 minutes. Transfer to a serving dish.

For a touch of chili flavor that does not overpower the whole dish, cut 1 to 2 dried chilies lengthwise, scrape away the seeds and fibers and add them to the hot sesame oil before the tofu skin. A sprinkling of Sichuan Pepper-Salt Powder (page 7) over the finished dish, plus a handful of chopped scallions, will also spice it up nicely without smothering the subtle flavors of the main ingredients.

Snow Peas and Shiitake Mushrooms Stir-fried with Ginger and Scallions

Snow peas are one of the favorite vegetables of Chinese cooks. Snow peas and mushrooms are a classic combination in Chinese cuisine because they harmonize *yin* and *yang* qualities. This dish may be prepared with either fresh or dried mushrooms. If you like it hot, add a few fresh or dried chilies (cut lengthwise with seeds and fibers removed) to the oil before cooking the mushrooms, and let them scorch before adding the mushrooms. You may also prepare this dish exactly the same way with broccoli instead of snow peas but make sure that you peel the broccoli stalks first. Another variation in flavor is to add a whole star anise along with the mushrooms and ginger.

$1/_2$ lb (225 g) fresh snow peas
$1/_2$ lb (225 g) fresh *shiitake* mushrooms, or 20 dried mushrooms
3 tablespoons oil
1 in ($2^1/_2$ cm) fresh ginger, minced
4 scallions, cut into 1-in ($2^1/_2$ cm) pieces

Sauce
$1^1/_2$ tablespoons soy sauce
$1^1/_2$ tablespoons rice wine
1 teaspoon sugar
$1/_2$ teaspoon salt
1 teaspoon sesame oil

Serves 4
Preparation time: **20 mins**
Cooking time: **5 mins**

1 Wash the snow peas, snap off the tips, and pull off the strings.

2 Wipe the mushrooms with a damp cloth to remove any grit, cut away stems, and cut in half, if large. If using dried mushrooms, soak in hot water for 15 minutes and drain; trim away the stems and cut each mushroom into four slices.

3 Combine all the Sauce ingredients and set aside.

4 Heat 2 tablespoons oil in a wok over medium heat, add the snow peas, and stir-fry until they turn bright green, about 1 minute. Remove from the heat and set aside.

5 Heat remaining oil in wok and, when hot, add the mushrooms and ginger. Stir-fry about 2 minutes, add the Sauce mixture, and cook for 1 minute more.

6 Add the snow peas and the scallions and stir-fry for 1 more minute. Transfer to a serving dish.

Stir-fried Green Beans with Bean Sprouts and Fresh Chilies

2 tablespoons oil
1 onion, thinly sliced
2 cloves garlic, minced
1 lb (450 g) green
  beans, trimmed and
  cut into 1$\frac{1}{4}$-in (3-cm)
  lengths
2 slices fresh ginger,
  julienned
1 large fresh red chili,
  seeded and cut into
  thin strips
$\frac{1}{4}$ teaspoon salt
1 teaspoon soy sauce
1 tablespoon rice wine
2 cups (200 g) fresh
  bean sprouts
2 teaspoon vinegar
2 teaspoon sesame oil
Fresh coriander leaves
  for garnish
Freshly ground black
  pepper, to taste

1 Heat the oil in a wok until very hot and stir-fry the onion, garlic, string beans, ginger, and chilies for 30 seconds. Add the salt, soy sauce, and wine and stir-fry for another 4 to 5 minutes.

2 Add the bean sprouts and stir-fry 1 minute. Add the vinegar and cook another 30 seconds. Add the sesame oil, stir to mix, remove from the heat, and transfer to platter and garnish with fresh coriander leaves. Sprinkle pepper to taste.

Serves 4
Preparation time: **20 mins**
Cooking time: **15 mins**

Savory Seared Runner Beans

3 tablespoons dried shrimps, soaked in warm water 10 mins
$^1/_2$ cup (125 ml) plus 2 tablespoons oil
1 lb (450 g) fresh runner or green beans, strings removed
5 cloves garlic, minced
3 slices fresh ginger, minced
3 scallions, chopped
1 tablespoon vinegar

Sauce
2 tablespoons rice wine
1 tablespoon water
1 teaspoon salt
1 tablespoon sugar

1 Combine the Sauce ingredients in a small bowl.
2 Drain the dried shrimps and chop finely. Set aside.
3 Heat $^1/_2$ cup oil in a wok until hot, add the long beans and fry until they begin to crinkle and become soft without burning. Remove and drain; discard the oil.
4 Heat remaining 2 tablespoons oil in the wok until hot, add the garlic, ginger, scallions, and shrimps and stir-fry for 30 seconds.
5 Add the beans and stir to coat them well in the oil, then add the sauce, and cook for about 3 minutes.
6 Turn off the heat, stir in the vinegar until blended, then remove to a serving dish.

Serves 4
Preparation time: **12 mins**
Cooking time: **10 mins**

Sautéed Chinese Peashoots with Garlic and Sichuan Pepper

1 lb (450 g) fresh
  Chinese peashoots
  (*dou miao*)
2 tablespoons oil
3 cloves garlic, minced
2 slices fresh ginger,
  julienned

Sauce
1 teaspoon salt
1 teaspoon sugar
$1/_2$ teaspoon ground
  Sichuan pepper
2 teaspoons rice wine
2 teaspoons sesame oil

1 Wash the peashoots carefully, and drain well. Remove and discard any wilted or yellowing leaves and tough stalks. Set aside.

2 Combine the Sauce ingredients and set aside.

3 Heat oil in a wok until hot, add the garlic and ginger and stir-fry quickly to release aromas, about 30 seconds. Add the peashoots, turning several times to coat evenly with oil, and immediately add the Sauce and continue to stir-fry for about 3 minutes, or until leaves turn a darker green. Remove to a platter and serve immediately.

Serves 4
Preparation time: **5 mins**
Cooking time: **5 mins**

Diced Vegetables Stir-fried with Ginger and Sichuan Pepper

2 ears corn

1 cup (120 g) fresh or frozen green peas

2 tablespoons oil

2 carrots, diced

1 green bell pepper, diced

1 onion, diced

5 oz (150 g) green beans, ends and strings removed and diced

1 in ($^1/_2$ cm) fresh ginger, minced

Sauce

1 teaspoon Sichuan Pepper-Salt Powder (page 7)

1 tablespoon soy sauce

1 tablespoon water

1 teaspoon sugar

$^1/_2$ teaspoon salt

1 teaspoon sesame oil

1 Shuck the corn and cut the kernels from the cob.

2 Heat the oil in a wok over medium heat, and stir-fry the corn, carrot, bell pepper, onion, string beans, and ginger for 2 minutes.

3 Add the peas, and continue to cook for another 1 or 2 minutes.

4 Add the Sauce and cook for 3 to 4 minutes, add the Sichuan powder and stir for 1 more minute to completely blend. Transfer to a serving dish.

Serves 4
Preparation time: **15 mins**
Cooking time: **10 mins**

Stir-fried Eggplant with Pungent Chili Sauce

4 Asian eggplants
 (about 1 lb or 450 g),
 stems removed
4 tablespoons oil

Chili Sauce
4 to 5 dried chilies
1 to 2 fresh red chilies,
 seeds removed
6 shallots, minced
2 cloves garlic, minced
2 tablespoons oil
$1/4$ cup (80 ml) Tamarind
 Juice (page 7)
2 teaspoons sugar
1 teaspoon salt

Serves 4
Preparation time: **15 mins**
Cooking time: **35 mins**

1 To make the Chili Sauce, cut dried chilies into thirds, and tap the seeds out. Soak in 1 cup warm water for 10 to 15 minutes until softened. Discard water and seeds.

2 Grind the soaked chilies, fresh chilies, shallots, and garlic in a spice grinder or blender and process until smooth, adding a little oil if needed to keep the mixture turning.

3 Heat oil in a wok over medium heat and stir-fry the chili paste, stirring frequently, until thoroughly cooked and oil surfaces, about 10 minutes. Add the Tamarind Juice, sugar, and salt and cook 1 minute. Set aside.

4 Cut each eggplant in half lengthwise. Heat half the oil in a skillet and fry half the eggplant until cooked and lightly browned, on both sides, about 10 minutes. Drain on absorbent paper. Heat remaining oil and cook the rest of the eggplant.

5 Put eggplant on a serving dish and spoon some Chili Sauce over the top of each piece.

If Asian eggplant is not available, use a regular eggplant weighing about 1 lb (450 g) and cut it crosswise in $1/2$-in (1-cm) thick slices, then cook as directed.

Sweet and Sour Eggplant

70 g ($2^1/_3$ oz) tamarind pulp soaked in 400 ml
  ($1^2/_3$ cups) water
4 large eggplants (aubergines), about 750 g ($1^1/_2$ lb)
250 ml (1 cup) mustard oil or other cooking oil
5 cloves
5 cardamoms
2 green chilies, slit lengthways
2 teaspoons chili powder
$^1/_2$ teaspoon turmeric powder
$^1/_2$ teaspoon cumin powder
1 tablespoon fennel powder
1 teaspoon *garam masala*
50 g ($^1/_4$ cup) caster sugar
Salt to taste

1 Stir, squeeze, and strain the tamarind pulp, discarding any solids, to obtain water.
2 Cut eggplants into quarters lengthways, then into 4-cm ($1^1/_2$-in) lengths.
3 Heat oil in a wok and fry the eggplants until half cooked. Drain and set aside.
4 Discard all but 2 tablespoons of the oil and fry the cloves, cardamoms, and green chilies until aromatic.
5 Add in the ground spice powders, salt, and sugar, tamarind water as well as the fried eggplant. Cook until the gravy has thickened and the eggplant tender.

Serves 4
Preparation time: **15 mins**
Cooking time: **15 mins**

Eggplant with Fragrant Meat Sauce

This dish makes use of a particular style of Sichuan seasoning that provides a highly aromatic blend of all the basic flavors—sweet, sour, salty, pungent, and bitter—in a sauce that has the subtle fragrance of the freshest seafood. To make this dish properly, you should use the long purple Asian eggplant. The traditional method of preparation uses your choice of ground meat, but you may substitute chopped *shiitake* mushrooms instead for a vegetarian version, or simply prepare it without meat or mushrooms.

$1/2$ cup plus 2 tablespoons vegetable oil
10 oz (300 g) Asian eggplants, about 4 medium ones, cut lengthwise, then quartered
6 cloves garlic, minced
8 slices fresh ginger, minced
$1/2$ cup fresh ground pork, beef, or lamb
1 tablespoon black bean chili paste
6 scallions, minced

Sauce
2 teaspoons soy sauce
2 teaspoons rice wine
1 teaspoon sesame oil
1 teaspoon vinegar
1 tablespoon sugar
$1/2$ teaspoon freshly ground black pepper
1 teaspoon salt
2 tablespoons water

1 Combine the Sauce ingredients and set aside.

2 Heat $1/2$ cup oil in a wok over high heat until hot, and add the eggplants. Stir-fry, turning frequently, until they change color and soften. Remove eggplant and set on a rack or colander to drain.

3 Heat the remaining 2 tablespoons oil until hot. Add the garlic and ginger and stir-fry for 1 minute. Add the ground meat and continue to stir-fry 2 more minutes. Add the black bean paste and chili paste and stir-fry 30 seconds. Add the Sauce mixture and stir to blend all ingredients.

4 Add the cooked eggplants and stir-fry until evenly coated. Cover with a lid, and simmer for 3 to 4 minutes, or until tender and fragrant. Remove to a serving dish and sprinkle with minced scallions.

Serves 4
Preparation time: **15 mins**
Cooking time: **10 mins**

Stir-fried Shredded Potatoes

Like chilies and tomatoes, white potatoes were introduced to China from the West, as reflected in the Chinese word, *yang yu*, which means "foreign taro." But like virtually all forms of food brought to China, the Chinese have applied their own culinary genius to the preparation of potatoes, which they neither deep-fry like the French, nor bake like the Americans. Instead of five-spice powder, you could try dusting the finished dish with some Sichuan Pepper-Salt Powder (page 7).

4 to 5 medium-sized white potatoes
3 tablespoons oil
1 teaspoon sugar
1 teaspoon salt
$^1/_2$ teaspoon five-spice powder
2 scallions, minced (optional)

Serves 4
Preparation time: **10 mins**
Cooking time: **10 mins**

1 Wash the potatoes well but do not peel them. Using a grater, shred the potatoes into a bowl of cool salted water to keep them from turning brown.
2 Just before cooking, strain the shredded potatoes, but do not rinse, and place in a colander to drain.
3 Heat the oil in a wok over medium until hot but not smoking.
4 Add the potatoes and stir-fry, then add the sugar, salt, and five-spice powder. Continue to cook over medium for 8 to 10 minutes, or until firm and tender. Add enough water as needed during cooking to prevent the potato from sticking to the pan.
5 Transfer to a serving plate and sprinkle evenly with the minced scallions.

Tomatoes Stir-fried with Onions and Pine Nuts

2 tablespoons oil
$^1/_2$ cup (100 g) white or yellow onion, diced
2 scallions, cut into $^1/_2$-in (1-cm) lengths
3 ripe tomatoes, cut into wedges
$^1/_3$ cup (50 g) pine nuts, toasted
$^1/_4$ teaspoon salt
1 teaspoon sugar
1 teaspoon soy sauce
Fresh coriander leaves for garnish

1 Heat oil in a wok over high heat until hot, and stir-fry the onions and scallions to release aromas, about 30 seconds.
2 Add the tomatoes, pine nuts, salt, sugar, and soy sauce, and stir-fry continuously for 1 to 2 minutes. Remove from heat, garnish with coriander leaves, and serve immediately.

Serves 4
Preparation time: **10 mins**
Cooking time: **5 mins**

Tofu, Green Beans, and Peanuts Stir-fried with Chili and Garlic

This is a very typical Chinese home-style dish, combining nourishing ingredients that are easily kept in stock in the kitchen and cooking them with a selection of stimulating seasonings that really help *shia fan* ("get the rice down"). For variety, add some diced carrots or green peas along with the green beans. If you have any leftovers, stir-fry it with leftover rice.

2 tablespoons oil
1 tablespoon sesame oil
10 oz (300 g) dried or firm tofu, cut into cubes
2 to 4 sliced red chilies, seeded and then sliced
10 oz (300 g) green beans, strings removed
6 to 8 cloves garlic, minced
1 in (2^1/$_2$ cm) fresh ginger, minced
1 cup (150 g) unsalted peanuts, skins removed
4 to 5 scallions, sliced

Sauce
1 tablespoon soy sauce
1 tablespoon rice wine
1 teaspoon sesame oil
1 teaspoon sugar
^{1}/$_2$ teaspoon salt

1 Mix the Sauce ingredients in a small bowl and set aside.
2 Heat the oils in a wok over medium heat and when hot, add the tofu and chili. Stir-fry for 1 minute, and add the green beans, garlic, and ginger, and stir-fry vigorously for 1 to 2 minutes more.
3 Add the peanuts and the Sauce mixture, and stir-fry for 2 minutes.
4 Stir in the scallions, then transfer to a serving dish.

Serves 4
Preparation time: **20 mins**
Cooking time: **5 mins**

Hot and Spicy Tofu

This dish is said to have been the speciality made by an old woman in a night market in Sichuan. Her dish was so renowned that people would travel from all over the province just to taste it. An equally tasty vegetarian version of this traditional recipe may be prepared with finely chopped *shittake* mushrooms.

1 cup (150 g) lean ground pork or lamb (about ¹/₃ lb)
2 cakes soft tofu (13 oz/400 g), drained
2 fresh red chilies, seeds removed and minced
6 cloves garlic, minced
6 slices fresh ginger, minced
3 tablespoons oil
1 tablespoon black bean paste
1 teaspoon red chili oil or chili paste
3 to 4 scallions, chopped
1 teaspoon Sichuan Pepper-Salt Powder (page 7)

Marinade
1 teaspoon cornstarch
¹/₂ teaspoon sugar
1 teaspoon soy sauce
1 tablespoon rice wine
1 teaspoon sesame oil
¹/₂ teaspoon ground Sichuan pepper

Sauce
1 cup (250 ml) water or chicken stock
1 tablespoon sugar
1 teaspoon salt
1 tablespoon soy sauce
1 teaspoon sesame oil

1 Combine the ground meat and Marinade ingredients in a bowl and set aside. Combine the Sauce ingredients and set aside. Cube the tofu, and finely chop the chilies, garlic, and ginger.

2 Heat oil in a wok over high heat and add the chilies, garlic, and ginger, then stir-fry for 1 minute. Add the ground meat and continue to stir-fry for 1 more minute. Add the bean paste, and chili oil or paste and cook for 1 minute more.

3 Add the Sauce, stir well to blend, and bring it to a boil. Add the tofu, stirring gently to coat with Sauce. Cover, reduce heat to medium, and cook for about 8 minutes, stirring occasionally to prevent sticking.

4 Uncover, stir gently to mix, and remove from the heat. Place in a serving bowl and sprinkle with chopped scallions and Sichuan Pepper-Salt Powder before serving.

Serves 4
Preparation time: **10 mins**
Cooking time: **10 mins**

Spicy Spinach Stir-fried with Tofu Skin

2 sheets dried tofu skin, soaked in water 20 minutes and drained
1 cup (2 clumps) dried white fungus (optional), soaked in water 30 minutes; drain
2 tablespoons oil
2 cloves garlic, crushed
3 slices fresh ginger
1 fresh red chili, halved lengthwise, seeded, and halved again
1 onion, thinly sliced
1 small carrot, peeled and thinly sliced
$^1/_2$ teaspoon salt
1 teaspoon sugar
2 tablespoons water
1 teaspoon vinegar
$^1/_2$ lb (225 g) spinach, rinsed well, stems removed and leaves cut into segments
1 teaspoon freshly ground black pepper
2 teaspoons sesame oil

1 Slice the soaked tofu skins into strips 2 x 1 in (5 x 2$^1/_2$ cm) wide. Shred the soaked fungus. Set aside.
2 Heat the oil in a wok over high heat until very hot, and stir-fry garlic, ginger, chilies, and onion for 2 minutes. Add the tofu skin, fungus, and carrot. Stir-fry for a further 1 to 2 minutes.
3 Stir in the salt, sugar, and 2 tablespoons of water. Cover with a lid, reduce heat to low, and cook for 6 minutes.
4 Add vinegar, stir to mix, and put in the spinach, black pepper, and sesame oil and stir-fry for another 3 minutes or until spinach is wilted and the stalks cooked through.

Serves 4
Preparation time: 20 mins + 30 mins soaking time
Cooking time: 15 mins

Tempe and Tofu Stir-fry

1½ oz (50 g) bean thread noodles, soaked in warm water 20 minutes and drained
6 to 8 tablespoons oil
5 oz (150 g) *tempe*, cubed
5 oz (150 g) firm tofu, cubed
3 cloves garlic, sliced
1 tablespoon fresh ginger, minced
½ teaspoon dried shrimp paste, toasted and crumbled
1 stalk lemongrass, crushed and cut into 2-in (5-cm) lengths
7 oz (200 g) medium shrimps, peeled and deveined
7 oz (200 g) green beans, tops, tails and strings removed, sliced diagonally
2 red chilies, seeds removed and sliced
1 teaspoon salt
3 tablespoons Tamarind Juice (page 7)
2 teaspoons palm sugar, crumbled

1 Cut noodles with scissors into shorter lengths.
2 Heat about 2 tablespoons oil in wok over high heat until hot, and stir-fry, stirring until golden brown, about 4 minutes. Drain on paper towels. Repeat with tofu.
3 Remove all but 2 tablespoons of oil from the wok. When oil is moderately hot, add garlic and ginger and stir-fry 20 seconds. Add shrimp paste and stir-fry, crumbling the shrimp paste.
4 Add the lemongrass and shrimps, and stir-fry for 2 minutes or until shrimps are cooked. Add the green beans, chili, *tempe*, and tofu. Stir-fry 2 minutes.
5 Add glass noodles, and salt. Stir-fry until beans are just tender, about 2 more minutes. Add Tamarind Juice, stir to mix well, and serve.

Serves 4
Preparation time: **35 mins**
Cooking time: **30 mins**

Spicy Stir-fried Rice Vermicelli

8 cups (2 liters) water
1 teaspoon salt
8 oz (250 g) dried rice
vermicelli
2 large eggs
Salt and freshly ground
black pepper to taste
4 tablespoons oil
2 cakes firm white tofu
$1^1/_2$ cups (300 g)
shrimps
1 cup (200 g) chicken
breast, cut into thin
strips
12 oz (330 g) bean
sprouts
3 cups (200 g) Chinese
chives, cut in 1-in
($2^1/_2$-cm) lengths
1 tablespoon sugar

Seasoning Paste

1 to 2 fresh red chilies,
seeds removed
5 cloves garlic
5 shallots
1 tablespoon fermented
soybean paste

Garnish

3 tablespoons Crispy
Fried Shallots (page 7)
$2/_3$ cup (80 g) scallions,
cut into 1-in ($2^1/_2$ cm)
lengths
3 limes, cut in wedges

1 To make the Seasoning Paste, place chilies, garlic, shallots, and preserved soya beans in a blender, adding some water if necessary, and process until almost smooth. Set aside.

2 Bring water and salt to the boil in a large pan. Add the rice vermicelli and cook until tender but not soft, 2 to 5 minutes depending on brand of noodles. Drain and cool in a colander. Set aside.

3 Beat the eggs with a pinch of salt and pepper. Heat 1 teaspoon of the oil in a pan and add eggs. Working quickly, rotate the pan to allow the eggs to coat the pan, making a thin omelet. When the omelet is lightly browned, flip and cook the other side for 10 to 20 seconds. Fold omelet. Slice thinly and set aside.

4 Cut tofu into halves and blot with paper towel to absorb excess moisture. Heat remaining oil in the wok and stir-fry tofu until lightly browned. Remove to a plate and cool before cutting into $1/_4$-in ($1/_2$-cm) slices.

5 Over medium heat, fry the ground Seasoning Paste in the oil until well cooked and oil separates. Add the shrimps and chicken, stir-frying until firm and cooked. Add the tofu, 1 teaspoon salt, and the sugar and stir-fry for 3 more minutes.

6 Add the noodles and stir-fry for 5 minutes, or until the paste has spread evenly. Add the bean sprouts and chives. Cook until the vegetables are wilted but still crunchy, about 5 minutes. Taste and adjust seasoning if necessary, adding a little light soy sauce rather than salt, if noodles are bland.

7 Transfer noodles onto a serving platter and garnish with the omelet strips, fried shallots, scallions, and lime wedges. Serve immediately.

Serves 4
Preparation time: **30 mins**
Cooking time: **30 mins**

Rice Noodles with Chicken and Chinese Broccoli

- 1 lb (450 g) Chinese broccoli
- 5 tablespoons oil
- 12 oz (360 g) dried rice sticks, soaked in water for 20 minutes and drained
- 1 tablespoon thick soy sauce
- 1 large egg, beaten
- 3 cloves garlic, chopped
- $1/2$ lb (225 g) chicken or pork, thinly sliced, or shrimps, shelled and deveined
- 1 tablespoon yellow bean paste
- 1 to 2 tablespoons fish sauce
- $1^1/_2$ cups (375 ml) chicken stock
- 1 tablespoon cornstarch mixed with 2 tablespoons water
- $1/4$ teaspoon ground white pepper

1 Cut the Chinese broccoli into 2-in (5-cm) lengths. Peel the tough stems and cut to the same size as the leafy portions.

2 Heat 2 tablespoons of the oil in a wok over high heat. Add the noodles and soy sauce and stir-fry for about 30 seconds. Push the noodles to the sides of the pan and add the egg. Stir the egg and noodles together and transfer to a serving platter.

3 Add the remaining oil to the same pan and heat. Add the garlic and stir-fry until golden, then stir-fry the meat until it changes color. Stir in the bean sauce and the fish sauce.

4 Stir in the greens, chicken stock, and cornstarch mixture, and continue cooking and stirring until the sauce is transparent. Pour the mixture over the noodles and sprinkle with the white pepper.

Serves 4
Preparation time: **15 mins**
Cooking time: **10 mins**

Stir-fried Thai Noodles with Shrimps

This dish may be prepared with meat or seafood instead of shrimps. Simply substitute 1 lb (450 g) mixed seafood, chicken, pork, or beef.

4 tablespoons vegetable oil
4 shallots, chopped
4 large eggs
1 lb (450 g) medium shrimps, peeled and deveined
7 oz (200 g) dried rice sticks, softened in water
$^1/_2$ cup (125 ml) Tamarind Juice (page 7)
1 tablespoons sugar
1 tablespoons fish sauce
1 tablespoons oyster sauce
1 tablespoons light soy sauce
1 teaspoon ground white pepper
3 cups (360 g) bean sprouts
$^2/_3$ cup (80 g) scallions, cut into 1-in (2$^1/_2$ cm) lengths
4 tablespoons ground roasted peanuts
2 limes, halved

1 Heat the oil in the wok over medium heat, add the shallots and egg. Stir-fry, then add shrimps, and continue stir-frying.
2 Add the rice noodles, stir-fry until soft, and add the Tamarind Juice, sugar, fish sauce, oyster sauce, soy sauce, and the ground pepper.
3 Add half the bean sprouts and half of the chives; mix well and dish onto 4 plates.
4 Serve hot garnish with the bean sprouts, chives, peanuts, and lime.

Serves 4
Preparation time: **10 mins**
Cooking time: **10 mins**

Stir-fried Rice Sticks with Beef in Soy Gravy

2 tablespoons oil
2 cloves garlic, chopped
$1/4$ lb (110 g) lean ground beef
1 large egg
$1/2$ cup (30 g) young corn kernels
$1/2$ cup (30 g) cauliflower florets
$1/2$ cup (20 g) asparagus, cut into 2-in (5-cm) slices
$1/2$ cup (20 g) Chinese broccoli, cut into 2-in (5-cm)
  lengths
7 oz (200 g) dried rice sticks, soaked in water for
  10 minutes and drained
1 tablespoon fish sauce
1 tablespoon oyster sauce
$1/2$ teaspoon sugar
1 teaspoon dark soy sauce
2 pinches ground white pepper

1 Heat the vegetable oil in a wok over medium heat, add the garlic, and stir-fry. Add the beef and stir-fry until browned.
2 Add the egg and stir well. Add all the vegetables and the noodles and stir-fry for 3 to 4 minutes, or until the vegetables are cooked.
3 Stir in the fish sauce, oyster sauce, sugar, soy sauce, and ground white pepper. Stir well, and serve immediately.

Serves 4
Preparation time: **1 hour**
Cooking time: **10 mins**

Malaysian-style Fried Egg Noodles

2 cakes firm white tofu
3 tablespoons oil
1 onion, thinly sliced
4 cloves garlic, chopped
$1/_2$ cup (100 g) chicken breast, cut into thin strips
$1/_2$ cup (100 g) shrimps, shelled and deveined
1 tomato, cut into wedges
2 cups (300 g) cabbage, thinly sliced
3 cups (150 g) mustard greens or *bok choy*, cut in $1^1/_2$-in (4-cm) pieces
1 lb (450 g) fresh wheat noodles, rinsed
2 large eggs
2 to 3 tablespoons Crispy Fried Shallots (page 7)
$2/_3$ cup (80 g) chives or scallions, cut into 1-in ($2^1/_2$-cm) lengths
1 large lime, cut in wedges

Sauce

1 tablespoon light soy sauce
1 tablespoon dark soy sauce
2 tablespoons tomato ketchup
1 teaspoon salt
2 teaspoons sugar

Chili Paste

2 tablespoons oil
6 dried chilies, sliced, soaked and drained
5 shallots, minced
5 cloves garlic, minced
1 teaspoon shrimp paste

1 To make the Sauce, combine all the Sauce ingredients in a bowl and set aside.

2 To prepare Chili Paste, combine chilies, shallots, garlic, and shrimp paste in a blender, adding some water and process until smooth. Heat the oil in a wok over medium heat and stir-fry the mixture until cooked and oil separates. Transfer to a bowl and clean wok.

3 Cut tofu into halves and blot with paper towel to absorb excess moisture. Heat oil in a wok over medium heat and stir-fry tofu until lightly browned on all sides. Remove from heat, place tofu on paper towels, and when cool enough to handle, cut into $1/_4$-in ($1/_2$-cm) thick slices. Leave remaining oil in the wok for frying the noodles.

4 Reheat the oil and stir-fry the onion and garlic for 2 minutes, or until fragrant. Add chicken and shrimps, stir-fry for 3 minutes, and add the tomato, cabbage, and mustard greens. Increase heat to high and stir-fry for 2 minutes. Stir in the chili paste and tofu and cook for 2 minutes more. Pour in Sauce mixture and noodles and stir-fry over high heat for 3 to 4 minutes.

5 Spread the noodles out into a flat layer. Make a well in the center of the noodles and drizzle in 2 teaspoons oil. Add 2 eggs, stirring to scramble. Stir-fry eggs and let eggs set and brown slightly. Combine all ingredients together and serve, garnished with fried shallots and scallions. Squeeze lime juice over noodles before eating.

Serves 4
Preparation time: **20 mins**
Cooking time: **20–30 mins**

Black Hokkien Noodles

1 lb (450 g) fresh or dried wheat noodles or fresh
Japanese *udon* noodles
3 tablespoons oil
5 cloves garlic, roughly chopped
$^3/_4$ cup (150 g) chicken breast, thinly sliced
$^3/_4$ cup (150 g) medium shrimps, shelled and deveined
$^1/_2$ cup (150 g) fresh squid, cut into 1-in ($2^1/_2$-cm)
  pieces
3 cups mustard greens, cut in 2-in (4-cm) lengths
1 cup round or Chinese cabbage, sliced $^1/_4$-in ($^1/_2$-cm)
  thick

Sauce
$2^1/_2$ tablespoons dark soy sauce
1 tablespoon light soy sauce
1 tablespoon oyster sauce
2 teaspoons sugar
$^1/_2$ teaspoon salt
$^1/_4$ teaspoon ground pepper
2 teaspoons cornstarch
1 cup (250 ml) water

1 Mix all the Sauce ingredients together in a bowl
and set aside. Bring 6 cups ($1^1/_2$ liters) water to boil in
a pan. Add the noodles, let the water boil again and
cook for 3 to 4 minutes or until the noodles are tender.
Drain, rinse in cold water, and drain in a colander.
2 Heat oil in a wok over high heat and stir-fry the
garlic until golden brown. Add the chicken and
shrimps and stir-fry for 2 minutes before adding the
squid. Cook for 1 to 2 minutes. Pour in the Sauce and
bring to the boil. Add the noodles and cook for 5 to
7 minutes. Add the vegetables and stir-fry for 2 to
3 minutes. Remove from the heat and serve.
3 Prepare Shrimp Paste Dip (page 7) and serve in
small sauce plates to accompany the noodles.

Serves 4
Preparation time: **30 mins**
Cooking time: **20 mins**

Stir-fried Bean Thread Noodles

4 tablespoons oil
3 cloves garlic, chopped
$^1/_2$ lb (250 g) thinly sliced pork, beef or chicken
3 tablespoons wood ear mushrooms, soaked in hot
  water for 20 minutes, and stems removed
1 carrot, peeled and julienned
1 stalk celery, shredded
7 oz (200 g) package bean thread noodles, soaked
  20 minutes, drained, and cut into 2-in (5-cm) lengths
$^1/_4$ cup (60 ml) chicken stock or cold water
2 large eggs, lightly beaten
1 tablespoon vinegar
3 tablespoons fish sauce
1 teaspoon sugar
$^1/_2$ teaspoon salt
$^1/_2$ teaspoon freshly ground black pepper
2 scallions, cut into 1-in (2$^1/_2$-cm) lengths

1 Heat 3 tablespoons oil in a wok over medium-high
heat. Stir-fry the garlic until light brown, 2 to 3 minutes. Add the meat, and stir-fry until the meat cooks
through, 2 to 3 minutes.
2 Add the mushrooms, carrots, and celery. Stir until well
mixed. Stir in the noodles, then the stock and mix
well. Push the noodles up onto the sides of the pan.
3 Add the remaining oil. Pour in the eggs and scramble
them, then mix with the contents of the pan. Stir in the
vinegar, fish sauce, sugar, salt, pepper, and scallions.
Remove to a serving platter.

Serves 2
Preparation time: **10 mins**
Cooking time: **15 mins**

Brown Rice with Mixed Vegetables

This is a good way to use leftover rice, particularly brown rice, which does not get as soggy as white rice. You may use almost any combination of vegetables — such as turnip, bell peppers, cooked corn, fresh mushrooms, chopped cabbage, diced squash — to prepare this dish, and it may stand alone as a meal. This is a typical example of the pragmatic spirit of Asian homestyle cooking, which always regards leftovers as the foundation of another good meal.

10 dried or fresh *shiitake* mushrooms
3 tablespoons oil
1 onion, sliced into crescents
3 to 4 cloves garlic, minced
3 to 4 slices fresh ginger, minced
2 carrots, diced
12 florets broccoli, stems peeled and cut into bite-sized pieces
1 green bell pepper, diced
1 cup fresh or frozen peas
3 cups cooked rice, white or brown
$1/2$ cup mushroom-soaking water

Sauce
1 tablespoon soy sauce
1 teaspoon rice wine
$1/2$ teaspoon sugar
1 teaspoon salt
1 teaspoon sesame oil

1 If using dried mushrooms, soak for 15 minutes in hot water, drain and reserve $1/2$ cup of the liquid. Remove the stems. Squeeze excess moisture from the mushrooms and slice each one into 4 to 6 strips.
2 Combine all the Sauce ingredients in a bowl and set aside.
3 Heat oil in a wok over high heat and stir-fry the mushrooms, onions, garlic, and ginger for 1 minute. Add the Sauce mixture, then add the carrots, broccoli, bell pepper, and peas. Stir-fry for 3 minutes.
4 Add rice and continue to cook until all ingredients are well mixed, then add the mushroom water and mix through until well combined.
5 Reduce heat, cover with lid, and cook for 3 to 4 minutes, then transfer to serving platter.

Serves 4
Preparation time: **20 mins**
Cooking time: **15 mins**

Seafood Fried Rice in Pineapple

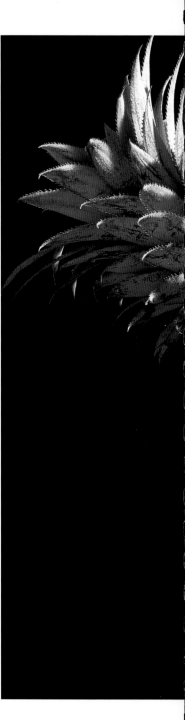

$^1/_2$ lb (225 g) squid
$^1/_2$ lb (225 g) small shrimps, shelled and deveined
4 oz (100 g) crab meat, picked clean
4 tablespoons oil
6 cups (800 g) cooked long-grain rice
$^1/_2$ cup (80 g) diced fresh pineapple
1 onion, diced
1 green or red bell pepper, diced
4 tablespoons yellow raisins
1 tablespoon curry powder
1 teaspoon sugar
2 tablespoons soy sauce
$^3/_4$ teaspoon ground white pepper
1 small tomato, diced
1 large fresh pineapple

1 To clean the squid, rinse under cold water, and pull the head from the body. Discard the head with its tentacles, reserving only the body. Pull the long quill from the body. Press out the innards by rubbing the body sac to be sure you have removed all of the gelatinous inner matter. Peel off the outer skin and slice the body lengthwise into thin strips.
2 With the sharp point of a knife, mark a 3 x 6-in $(7^1/_2$ x 15-cm) rectangular outline on one side of the pineapple. Then, cut into the pineapple along these lines, angling the knife inwards so as to cut a pyramid-shaped hollow out of the fruit.
3 Heat the oil in the wok over high heat, add seafood, rice, pineapple, onion, pepper, and raisins and stir-fry until well mixed, about 8 to 10 minutes. Add the curry powder, sugar, soy sauce, pepper, and tomato, and stir-fry for another 1 minute.
4 Serve the Fried Rice in the hollow that has been created in the pineapple.

Serves 4
Preparation time: 30 mins
Cooking time: 10 mins

Fragrant Shrimp Fried Rice

The idea of stir-frying rice with other ingredients originated in China and has made its way throughout Asia. Generally, a serving of fried rice with all the trimmings makes a filling meal; this version is very light and delicate. Note that using cold rice works best for stir-frying because the grains separate easily.

3 tablespoons oil
2 cloves garlic, minced
8 oz (225 g) shrimps, peeled and deveined
1 small onion, peeled and sliced
1 ripe tomato, cut into 8 sections
2 large eggs, lightly beaten
4 cups (550 g) cooked long-grain rice
1 scallion, chopped
1 sprig fresh coriander, coarsely chopped

Seasoning
1 tablespoon soy sauce
1 tablespoon fish sauce
1/2 teaspoon salt
1/4 teaspoon freshly ground white pepper

1 To make the Seasoning, mix all the ingredients in a small bowl.

2 Heat oil in a wok over medium heat. Add the garlic and stir-fry about 1 minute.

3 Add the shrimps and cook 2 to 3 minutes. Add the onion and tomato and stir several times. Push the contents to the sides, making a well in the center.

4 Add the eggs, stirring quickly to prevent cooking through. Add the rice, mix well, and continue to cook and stir until the mixture is heated through.

5 Add the Seasoning to the rice. Stir a few times until all the ingredients are well combined, and add the chopped scallion. Remove to a platter and garnish with fresh coriander.

Serves 2–3
Preparation time: **10 mins**
Cooking time: **8 mins**

Home-style "Leftovers" Fried Rice

Fried rice is probably the single most commonly prepared dish in kitchens of Asian homes, and it is rarely prepared from scratch. Instead, it utilizes leftover rice along with leftover vegetables, tofu, meat scraps, and other items to prepare a tasty hot meal that is quick and easy to cook, requiring no shopping. You may allow your culinary creativity to express itself freely when cooking fried rice at home, while also applying the "waste not, want not" philosophy of the Asian kitchen.

Assorted leftover ham, chicken, or bacon, tofu and vegetables (except leafy greens), such as carrot, corn, mushroom, peas, green beans, and onion
$1/4$ cup oil
3 to 4 cloves garlic, minced
1 chili pepper, seeded and thinly sliced
1 large egg, lightly beaten
3 to 4 cups cooked rice, white or brown
4 to 5 scallions, minced
1 teaspoon salt
1 teaspoon freshly ground black pepper

Serves 4
Preparation time: **15 mins**
Cooking time: **10 mins**

1 Chop all meat and vegetable leftovers into small pieces, then set aside in a bowl.
2 Heat oil in a wok over medium-high heat. When hot, add the garlic, chili, and leftovers and stir-fry quickly for about 1 minute.
3 Add the egg, stirring quickly to scramble. Add the rice and continue to stir-fry until the rice and vegetables are well mixed, until the rice begins to brown, about 3 to 5 minutes.
4 Sprinkle on the scallions, salt, and pepper, and continue to stir and turn for another 1 to 2 minutes. Transfer to serving dish, or to individual rice bowls.

The cooked rice should be dry and firm when preparing this dish; soggy rice does not work well in this recipe. If you have leftover meats as well, such as stir-fried fish, they may be added along with the vegetables and tofu. A sprinkling of chopped fresh coriander and a dusting of Sichuan Pepper-Salt Powder (page 7) on top of the finished dish provide some stimulating flavors that add a lot of character.

Classic Chicken, Pork, or Beef Thai Fried Rice

Tightly covered and refrigerated, the Chili Dipping Sauce will keep for up to 2 weeks. It can be spooned over just about any dish: soups, salads, grilled meats, fish, noodles, and curries. Use a dry spoon.

4 cups (500 g) cooked long-grain rice
4 tablespoons oil
5 cloves garlic, minced
$1/2$ lb (225 g) chicken breast, pork loin, or beef (sirloin, round, or flank steak), cut into thin strips
2 large eggs
4 tablespoons soy sauce
$1/2$ teaspoon ground white pepper
1 tablespoon light brown sugar
5 scallions, green tops only, thinly sliced
$1/2$ cup fresh coriander leaves
1 cucumber, peeled, quartered and sliced
2 tomatoes, cut into wedges
1 lime, quartered

Chili Dipping Sauce
$1/2$ cup (125 ml) fresh lime juice
3 tablespoons fish sauce
3 chilies, thinly sliced
2 cloves garlic, minced

1 To make the Chili Dipping Sauce, combine all of the ingredients in a small serving bowl. This makes $3/4$ cup (175 ml).
2 Put the cooked rice in a large bowl and toss it gently with your hands to separate the grains. Set aside.
3 Heat a wok over medium-high heat. Add the oil, making sure to coat the sides of the wok. When the oil is hot, add the garlic and stir-fry for 1 minute.
4 Add the meat. Stir-fry for about 1 minute.
5 Break the eggs into the wok and stir-fry for another 45 seconds. Add the rice and stir-fry, pressing the rice down on the bottom of the wok; turn the rice over and continue to stir-fry 3 more minutes.
6 Add the soy sauce, sugar, and pepper, and stir-fry for 1 minute more. Garnish with the scallions, and serve with cucumbers, tomatoes, lime quarters, and Chili Dipping Sauce.

Serves 4
Preparation time: **20 mins**
Cooking time: **12 mins**

Indian Fried Rice

3 tablespoons oil
1 tablespoon fresh
  ginger, minced
1 cup (100 g) onion,
  diced
1 tablespoon curry
  powder
$1/2$ lb (225 g) chicken or
  lamb, sliced into thin
  strips
2 cups (400 g) fresh
  tomatoes, diced
1 cup (100 g) fresh or
  frozen peas
Salt and freshly ground
  pepper to taste
4 cups (600 g) cooked
  rice, cooled
2 tablespoons mint
  leaves or parsley,
  chopped

1 Heat oil in a wok over medium heat and stir-fry the ginger and onion until fragrant. Add curry powder and stir-fry for about 2 minutes until aromatic.

2 Add the chicken or lamb strips and stir-fry over high heat for 2 minutes.

3 Add the tomatoes, peas, salt, pepper, and rice and stir-fry for about 5 minutes. Garnish with mint leaves or parsley and serve.

Leftover roast meat can be used as a substitute for fresh meat. If fresh diced tomatoes are unavailable, you can use 2 tablespoons tomato purée or ketchup. Cooked rice should be fluffy; overnight or leftover rice is ideal.

Serves 4
Preparation time: **15 mins**
Cooking time: **10 mins**

Fish Stir-fried with Black Beans and Pepper

You may use any type of firm-fleshed, salt water fish for this recipe — such as tuna, halibut, snapper, sea bass, or swordfish. Different types of fish cook at slightly different rates, and the size of the pieces also influence cooking time — so be careful not to overcook, as that will make the fish tough. This dish may be garnished with chopped fresh coriander leaves.

1⅓ lb (600 g) fish
  steaks or fillets
3 tablespoons oil
3 to 4 cloves garlic,
  minced
1½ to 2 tablespoons
  black bean paste
6 scallions, cut into
  1-in (2½-cm) sections
1 teaspoon sugar
1 teaspoon freshly
  coarsely ground black
  pepper
Fresh coriander leaves as
  garnish (optional)

Marinade
2 tablespoons rice wine
1 teaspoon sesame oil
3 tablespoons fresh
  ginger, minced

1 Cut the fish into chunks. If using steaks, remove bones. Place fish in a mixing bowl.

2 Mix the Marinade ingredients, pour over fish, and turn to coat the fish evenly. Cover and set aside to marinate for about 30 minutes.

3 Heat the oil in a wok over high heat, and add the marinated fish and garlic. Stir-fry for 1 to 2 minutes, until fish changes color. Add the black bean paste and continue to cook for another 1 to 2 minutes.

4 Add the scallions, sugar, and black pepper, stirring for 1 more minute to blend the flavors. Transfer to a serving dish.

Serves 4
Preparation time: **30 mins**
Cooking time: **5 mins**

Vietnamese Caramel Fish

The Vietnamese typically use catfish for this dish, but any firm-fleshed fish will do. Use whole fish or large slices of cross-cut fillets as these keep whole better. The fish is delicious served over steamed rice.

1½ lb (675 g) catfish fillets
2 tablespoons oil
4 thin slices fresh ginger, julienned

Sauce
²/₃ cup (160 g) sugar
½ cup (140 ml) fish sauce
8 shallots, peeled and thinly sliced
½ teaspoon freshly ground black pepper

1 To make the Sauce, cook the sugar in a saucepan over low heat until it starts to melt and caramelize. Remove the pan from the heat and add the fish sauce. This causes the sauce to bubble vigorously.
2 Return the pan to the heat and bring to a boil. Stir often to prevent the sugar mixture from scorching. Cook until it turns syrupy, about 4 minutes. Add the shallots and black pepper and stir well to combine. Remove the pan from the heat and cool the sauce. Makes about ²/₃ cup (170 ml) sauce
3 Slice the fish. Heat the oil in a wok over medium heat. Add the fish and fry for 2 to 3 minutes on each side. Add the ginger and Sauce and bring the mixture to the boil.
4 Reduce the heat to low and cook another 2 to 3 minutes, or until the fish is done. Remove from the heat and place on a serving platter.

Serves 4–6
Preparation time: **10 mins**
Cooking time: **25 mins**

Stir-fried Sliced Fish with Ginger

The perfect duo, fresh ginger and mushrooms, perk up this stir-fried fish. For the snappiest flavor, look for young fresh ginger.

1 lb (450 g) flounder or other white fish
3 tablespoons oil
3 cloves garlic, minced
6 slices (about $1/3$ cup) fresh ginger, julienned
3 fresh *shiitake* mushrooms, stems removed, tops sliced into thin strips
1 tablespoon black bean sauce
$1/4$ cup (60 ml) chicken stock
2 teaspoons fish sauce
$1/2$ teaspoon freshly ground black pepper
1 teaspoon sugar
1 chili, sliced (optional)
2 scallions, sliced
1 sprig fresh coriander leaves, coarsely chopped

1 Cut the fish into bite-sized pieces. Set aside.
2 Heat the oil in a wok over medium heat. Stir-fry the garlic, ginger, and mushrooms for 2 to 3 minutes. Add the bean sauce and chicken stock and cook 3 to 5 minutes more or until mixture is bubbling. Stir in the fish slices and fry until fish is cooked through.
3 Add the fish sauce, black pepper, sugar and chilies, if desired, and mix well. Remove from the heat and place on a serving platter. Garnish with the scallions and fresh coriander and serve.

Serves 4–6
Preparation time: **8 mins**
Cooking time: **10 mins**

Bengali Fish Curry

4 tablespoons oil
1 lb (450 g) fish slices
$1/2$ teaspoon cumin seeds
$1/4$ teaspoon fenugreek
$1/4$ teaspoon fennel
$1/4$ teaspoon mustard seeds
3 tablespoons ginger paste
3 tablespoons garlic paste
3 tablespoons green chili paste
1 teaspoon turmeric powder
3 tablespoons mustard seeds, ground
Scant 1 cup (200 ml) water
1 teaspoon salt

1 Heat half the oil and fry the fish slices for 3 minutes on both sides. Drain and set aside with the oil and the juice.
2 In a large saucepan or wok, heat remaining oil and fry the cumin, fenugreek, fennel, and mustard seeds until aromatic. Add in the rest of the ingredients except for the fried fish slices and cook for 5 minutes, stirring often.
3 When the gravy bubbles, gently lower the fish slices into the pan and simmer for 3 minutes. Remove and serve.

Serves 4
Preparation time: **10 mins**
Cooking time: **25 mins**

Sichuan Shrimps with Chili Sauce

Shrimps are one of most popular seafoods throughout the world, but no one cooks them better than Chinese chefs. In this Sichuan version, they are marinated in ginger and wine, then cooked very quickly with garlic, scallions, and a savory chili sauce. For best results, use fresh shrimps but frozen shrimps may also be used as long as they are top quality and fresh frozen.

1 lb (450 g) fresh or
  frozen raw shrimps,
  shelled and deveined
2 tablespoons oil
3 to 4 cloves garlic,
  minced
4 scallions, cut in $2^1/_2$-in
  (6-cm) lengths

Marinade
2 tablespoons rice wine
1 teaspoon sesame oil
1 tablespoon ginger,
  minced
$^1/_2$ teaspoon sugar

Sauce
2 tablespoons chili sauce
1 teaspoon tomato
  ketchup
$^1/_2$ teaspoon sugar
1 teaspoon salt
1 teaspoon sesame oil
2 teaspoons cornflour
  dissolved in 125 ml
  ($^1/_2$ cup) water

1 Place the shrimps in a bowl. Combine the Marinade ingredients, stir, then pour over the shrimps, mixing well with a spoon or fingers. Set aside to marinate for 15 to 20 minutes.
2 Combine the Sauce ingredients and set aside.
3 Heat oil in a wok until hot. Add the garlic and the marinated shrimps and stir-fry swiftly until the shrimps turn pink and the flesh becomes firm, about 1 to 2 minutes. Add the sauce and stir-fry for a further 1 minute to mix the ingredients.
4 Add the scallions and cook for 30 seconds more, then remove to platter, and serve immediately.

Serves 4
Preparation time: **30 mins**
Cooking time: **5 mins**

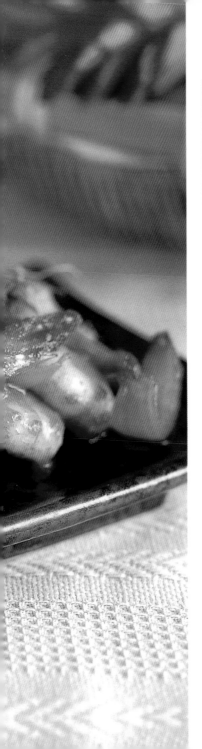

Tangy Tamarind Shrimps

10 shallots, chopped
4 tablespoons oil
1 to 1¹/₄ lb (450–600 g) medium shrimps, peeled, deveined and tails left intact
3 kaffir lime leaves, edges slightly torn
1 onion, cut in 10 wedges
2 teaspoons sugar
1 teaspoon salt

Spice Paste
5 to 10 dried chilies, cut into thirds
¹/₂ cup (125 ml) Tamarind Juice (see page 7)
¹/₂ teaspoon dried shrimp paste, toasted and crumbled

1 To make the Spice Paste, soak the chilies in hot water until soft, 10 to 15 minutes. Rub with the hands to remove as many seeds as possible.
2 To make the Spice Paste, grind the chilies, shrimp paste, and shallots in a spice grinder, or mortar and pestle, until smooth, adding a little oil if necessary to keep mixture turning.
3 Heat the oil in a wok over medium heat and add the chili mixture. Stir-fry 6 to 8 minutes, until the oil surfaces.
4 Add Tamarind Juice, reduce the heat to medium–low, and cook, stirring frequently, for 10 minutes. Add the shrimp, kaffir lime leaves, and onion wedges, increase the heat to medium, and stir-fry 5 minutes. Add sugar and salt and stir until dissolved. Serve.

Serves 4
Preparation time: 30 mins
Cooking time: 30 mins

Shrimp Masala

3 tablespoons oil
2 teaspoons cumin
  seeds
2 onions, diced
3 tablespoons ginger,
  grated
2 cloves garlic, crushed
2 tablespoons lemon
  juice or vinegar
1 tablespoon palm
  sugar, shaved
3 ripe tomatoes, diced
1 teaspoon *garam
  masala*
1 teaspoons cayenne
  pepper
1 teaspoon ground
  turmeric powder
$1/2$ teaspoon ground
  nutmeg powder
$1/2$ teaspoon freshly
  ground black
  pepper
1 teaspoon salt
1 lb (450 g) shrimps,
  shelled and deveined
2 tablespoons fresh
  coriander leaves,
  chopped

1 Heat the oil and fry the cumin seeds until aromatic then add the onions and sauté until golden brown.
2 Stir in the remaining ingredients except for the shrimps and coriander leaves and continue cooking over low heat until the oil separates.
3 Add the shrimps and stir to mix well. Cover and leave to simmer until the shrimps are cooked through, about 10 minutes.
4 Sprinkle with chopped coriander leaves and serve.

Serves 4
Preparation time: 30 mins
Cooking time: 20 mins

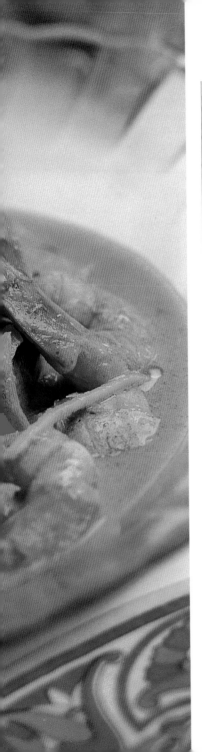

Shrimp Curry

1 1/2 lb (750 g) medium shrimps, shells removed and deveined
1 tablespoon cayenne pepper
2 tablespoons fish curry powder
1/2 teaspoon turmeric powder
1 tablespoon ginger, julienned
2 cloves garlic, minced
3 tablespoons oil
1/2 teaspoon mustard seeds
1 teaspoon cumin seeds
1 onion, thinly sliced
2 sprigs curry leaves
1 cup (250 ml) thick coconut milk
1 1/2 cups (300 g) cucumber, peeled, seeds removed, and cubed
2 green chilies, cut into 2-cm (1-in) lengths
1 tablespoon white vinegar or lime juice
Salt to taste

1 In a bowl, combine the shrimps, cayenne pepper, curry powder, and turmeric powder, ginger and garlic. Set aside for 5 minutes.
2 Heat the oil in a frying pan. Fry the mustard and cumin seeds until aromatic. Add the onion and curry leaves and sauté until the onion is golden brown. Add the prawns and sauté a further 4 minutes.
3 Add coconut milk, cucumber, chilies, and vinegar. Bring to the boil, and simmer gently, stirring continuously for 3 minutes. Add salt to taste.

Serves 4
Preparation time: **10 mins**
Cooking time: **10 mins**

Vietnamese-style Spicy Shrimps

1 lb (450 g) medium
shrimp, shelled and
deveined
12 cloves garlic, minced
1 tablespoon fish sauce
$1/_2$ teaspoon salt
3 tablespoons oil
2 red or green chilies,
minced
1 tablespoon oyster
sauce
2 sprigs fresh coriander
leaves, coarsely
chopped

1 Place the shrimp in a large mixing bowl and stir in
1 teaspoon chopped garlic, 1 tablespoon fish sauce
and the salt. Set aside for 30 minutes.
2 Heat the oil in a wok or frying pan over high heat,
add the shrimps, and stir-fry until they turn pink,
about 5 minutes. Remove to a serving platter.
3 Stir the chilies, the remaining fish sauce and garlic,
and the oyster sauce into the wok and cook over
high heat for about 1 minute. Pour over the shrimps,
garnish with the fresh coriander, and serve.

Serves 4
Preparation time: **10 mins**
Cooking time: **7 mins**

Crabs in Garlic and Pepper Sauce

3 lb (1¹/₂ kg) live crabs, plunged in boiling water to stun them
3 tablespoons oil
5 cloves chopped garlic, minced
1 tablespoon freshly ground black pepper
¹/₂ teaspoon salt
¹/₂ teaspoon sugar
3 scallions, thinly sliced
¹/₂ cup (125 ml) water or chicken stock

Serves 4–6
Preparation time: **15 mins**
Cooking time: **15 mins**

1 To clean the crabs, lift up the shell and if there is orange roe underneath, scoop it out and set aside. Cut off the tip of each leg, but leave the claws and legs attached. With a sharp cleaver, chop the crabs in half.

2 Heat the oil in a wok over high heat and stir-fry the garlic and pepper until fragrant, about 2 minutes. Add the crabs and stir-fry about 5 minutes before adding the salt, sugar, and scallions; stir-fry another 2 minutes. Sprinkle in half the water and stir before covering the wok. Cook another 8 or 10 minutes until the crab legs turn red. Add the rest of the water and stir-fry another 5 minutes more. Remove from the heat and serve.

Thai Mussels with Lemongrass

1 lb (450 g) mussels,
  cleaned
$^{1}/_{2}$ cup (125 ml) water
2 shallots, diced
1 stalk lemongrass,
  crushed and cut into
  2-in (5-cm) lengths
$^{1}/_{2}$ teaspoon salt
$^{1}/_{4}$ teaspoon freshly
  ground black pepper
$^{1}/_{2}$ cup (10 g) Asian
  basil leaves

Dipping Sauce
2 cloves garlic
2 fresh coriander roots
2 or 3 red chilies
$^{1}/_{2}$ cup (125 ml) water
$^{1}/_{2}$ cup (125 ml) fresh
  lime or lemon juice
$^{1}/_{4}$ cup (60 ml)
  fish sauce
1 teaspoon salt
1 tablespoon sugar
2 tablespoons fresh
  coriander leaves,
  chopped

1 To prepare the Dipping Sauce, use a pestle and mortar to pound the garlic, coriander roots, and chilies until smooth. Combine this paste with the remaining Dipping Sauce ingredients in a mixing bowl and stir well.

2 Discard any open mussels. Place the remainder in a wok and add the remaining ingredients. Cover and bring to a boil over high heat, cooking for 5 minutes. Remove from the heat and serve with the Dipping Sauce. To eat, remove the mussels from the shells and dip in the Sauce.

Serves 4 to 6
Preparation time: **15 mins**
Assembling time: **5 mins**

Seafood and Vegetable Stir-fry

$1/_2$ lb (225 g) fresh squid
1 carrot
$1/_2$ lb (225 g) fresh shrimps, shelled and deveined, or sea scallops
$1/_2$ cup (45 g) broccoli, cut into florets
6 oz (170 g) fresh green beans, tops, tails, and strings removed
2 tablespoons oil
1 onion, finely sliced
4 cloves garlic, minced
1 fresh red chili, cut diagonally into 3 or 4 pieces

Sauce
2 tablespoons soy sauce
3 tablespoons rice wine
1–2 teaspoons sugar
1 tablespoon sesame oil
$1^1/_2$ teaspoons corn-starch dissolved in $1/_2$ cup (125 ml) water

1 To clean the squid, remove the tentacles from the body and cut out the hard beaky portion. Remove the skin from the body of the squid, and clean inside, then cut into bite-sized pieces. Dry thoroughly. Clean cuttlefish and sea cucumber. Next, slice open the squid, cuttlefish, and sea cucumber lengthways and cut in half. Cut each piece into strips about $1/_4$ in ($1/_2$ cm) wide, place them in a bowl, and set aside.

2 Cut carrot in half lengthwise, then slice each half into pieces $1/_4$ in ($1/_2$ cm) wide.

3 Bring a large pot of water to a rolling boil, then blanch all vegetables for 3 minutes. Drain and set aside.

4 To make the Sauce, combine all ingredients and blend well. Set aside.

5 Heat oil in a wok over high heat until smoking. Add the onions, garlic, and chili and stir-fry to release their aromas, about 1 minute.

6 Add seafood and vegetables and continue to stir-fry until all the ingredients are well coated with oil, about 2 minutes.

7 Stir the Sauce to mix, then add to the wok and continue to stir-fry until Sauce is well blended with seafood and vegetables, for 2 to 3 minutes. Remove from heat, transfer to a platter, and serve.

Serves 4
Preparation time: **25 mins**
Cooking time: **10 mins**

Spicy Stir-fried Sichuan Squid

This type of dish belongs to a category of home-style Sichuan cooking known as *xiao chao*, which literally means "small fry." Squid has long been prized in Chinese family kitchens as an excellent yet inexpensive nutritional source of protein and essential minerals from the sea.

1 lb (450 g) fresh squid
1 tablespoon oil
5 to 6 cloves garlic, thinly sliced
4 slices fresh ginger
2 fresh red chilies, cut in $^1/_2$-in (1-cm) pieces
3 scallions, washed and cut into 1$^1/_2$-in (3-cm) pieces
2 stalks fresh celery, strings removed, washed and cut into 1$^1/_2$-in (3-cm) pieces
Salt to taste

Sauce
2 teaspoons rice wine
1 teaspoon sugar
1 tablespoon sesame oil
1 tablespoon thick soy sauce
1 tablespoon water

1 Combine the Sauce ingredients and set aside.
2 Remove the tentacles from the squid and cut out the hard beaky portion. Remove the skin from the body of the squid, and clean inside, then cut into bite-sized pieces. Dry thoroughly and set aside.
3 Heat the remaining oil in a wok over medium heat, add the garlic, ginger, and chilies, and stir-fry for about 2 minutes.
4 Increase heat to high, add the scallions, celery, and squid, and stir-fry for 1 minute. Add the Sauce mixture and continue to stir-fry for 3 to 4 minutes more. Remove to a platter and serve.

If thick black soy sauce is not available, add $^1/_2$ tablespoon brown sugar to 1 tablespoon regular soy sauce.

Serves 4
Preparation time: **15 mins + 2–3 hours soaking**
Cooking time: **15 mins**

Gung Bao Squid with Dried Chilies

Gung bao dishes are traditionally attributed to the private kitchen of a certain Duke of Bao in ancient Sichuan, whose personal chef was the reigning master of gourmet cuisine in his time. It involves first scorching dried red chilies in searing hot oil until they are almost black, then tossing in the main ingredients to "explode-fry" (*bao chao*) them quickly in pungent hot oil, and finishing it all off with a savory sauce.

1 whole squid, about
  1 lb (450 g)
3 tablespoons oil
5 dried red chilies, cut
  across in thirds
10 Sichuan peppercorns
3 slices fresh ginger, cut
  in thirds
2 scallions, cut in thirds

Sauce
1 tablespoon soy sauce
$1/2$ to 1 tablespoon
  sugar
1 tablespoon rice wine
1 teaspoon tomato
  ketchup
2 teaspoons vinegar
2 teaspoons sesame oil
2 teaspoons cornstarch
  dissolved in $1/2$ cup
  (125 ml) water

1 Lay the squid flat on a cutting board, and with a sharp knife, make diagonal cuts across the entire surface, cutting only about halfway into the flesh. Repeat same pattern at a 90-degree angle to the first cuts making cross-hatch marks $1/2$ inch (1 cm) apart. Then cut the squid into 1-in ($2^1/_2$-cm)-square or rectangular pieces.

2 To make the Sauce, combine the Sauce ingredients and set aside.

3 Heat the oil in wok over high heat until very hot. Add the chilies and scorch for 30 to 60 seconds, then add the Sichuan peppercorns, ginger, and scallions, and stir-fry swiftly to release the aromas, about 1 minute.

4 Add the drained squid to the wok and stir-fry for 30 to 60 seconds, then stir the Sauce mixture to mix ingredients and add to the squid. Stir-fry to blend all flavors for about 3 more minutes, then remove to a platter and serve.

Serves 4
Preparation time: **10 mins**
Cooking time: **10 mins**

Five-spice Chicken with Garlic and Scallions

You can also add $1/_2$ cup (60 g) fresh or frozen green peas after stir-frying the chicken for a minute or two. A sprinkling of chopped fresh coriander leaves on the finished dish goes very well with these flavors.

$2/_3$ lb (350 g) chicken breast, cubed
3 tablespoons sesame oil
5 to 6 cloves garlic, minced
4 scallions, cut into 1-in ($2^1/_2$-cm) pieces

Marinade
2 tablespoons rice wine
1 tablespoon soy sauce
1 teaspoon sesame oil
1 teaspoon sugar
$1/_2$ teaspoon salt
2 teaspoons five-spice powder
1 teaspoon cornstarch dissolved in 1 tablespoon water

1 Place the chicken in a bowl with the Marinade ingredients, stirring to coat the chicken well. Set aside for 15 to 20 minutes.
2 Drain the marinade, reserving all the liquid.
3 Heat the sesame oil and when hot, add the garlic and chicken, and stir-fry for 3 to 4 minutes, then add the reserved Marinade and scallions and cook for another 2 minutes. Transfer to a serving dish.

Serves 4
Preparation time: 20 mins
Cooking time: 6 mins

Stir-fried Cumin Chicken

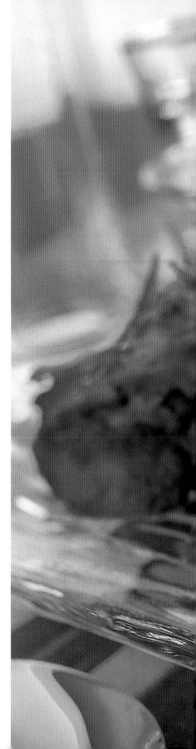

1$^{1}/_{2}$ to 2 lbs ($^{3}/_{4}$–1 kg) chicken pieces
1 teaspoon salt
Pinch of white pepper
1 tablespoon cumin seeds
1$^{1}/_{2}$ teaspoons fennel seeds
1 teaspoon black peppercorns
$^{3}/_{4}$-in (2-cm) piece fresh ginger
5 cloves garlic
3 tablespoons oil
1 cup (250 ml) water

1 Sprinkle chicken pieces with salt and pepper and set aside.
2 Dry-roast the cumin, fennel, and black peppercorns in a skillet over low heat until fragrant and crisp, about 2 minutes, taking care not to burn. Grind to a powder in an electric grinder or mortar and pestle. Set aside. Grind the ginger and garlic to a smooth paste. Set aside.
3 Heat the oil in a wok over medium heat and stir-fry the ginger and garlic, 30 seconds. Add the chicken pieces and stir-fry for 10 minutes over medium heat.
4 Add the ground spices and stir-fry for 10 minutes over medium heat.
5 Add water and bring to the boil. Turn down heat and simmer uncovered, stirring frequently, until chicken pieces are tender and most of the liquid has evaporated, 12 to 15 minutes.

Serves 4
Preparation time: **20 mins**
Cooking time: **35 mins**

Chicken with Coriander Yogurt Gravy

1 1/2 lbs (750 g) chicken, skin removed and cut into 8 pieces
1 teaspoon cayenne pepper
1 teaspoon salt
1 cup (250 ml) plain yogurt
2 tablespoons oil
2 1/2 cups (300 g) onions, diced
2 tablespoons fresh ginger, grated
2 tablespoons garlic, crushed
2 green chilies, seeds removed and minced
2 tablespoons ground coriander
1 teaspoon ground cumin
3 cups (200 g) fresh coriander leaves, chopped
1 1/2 cups (100 g) fresh mint leaves, chopped

1 Mix the chicken with the cayenne pepper, salt, and half the yogurt. Marinate for 15 minutes.

2 In a large wok, heat the oil over medium heat and stir-fry the onions until transparent. Add the ginger and garlic pastes and stir-fry until fragrant.

3 Add the green chilies, coriander, and cumin, stirring well into the onion mixture.

4 Remove the chicken pieces from the yogurt, add to the spice paste, stir-frying for 5 minutes.

5 Using a spatula, scrape the leftover marinade from the bowl over the chicken, adding the remaining 1/2 cup (125 ml) yogurt. Add the chopped coriander and mint leaves and mix well.

6 Bring to a simmering boil, cover, and reduce the heat to low and cook until chicken pieces are done about 15 minutes. Serve immediately.

Serves 4–6
Preparation time: 20 mins
Cooking time: 25 mins

Stir-fried Chicken with Asian Basil and Vegetables

2 tablespoons oil
3 cloves garlic, minced
3 bird's-eye chilies, minced
2 tablespoons green peppercorns
1 lb (450 g) chicken breast, cut into 2 x $\frac{1}{2}$-in
   (5 x 1-cm) strips
1$\frac{1}{2}$ cups (150 g) canned baby corn (optional)
10 cups dried *shiitake* mushrooms, soaked in water
   for 20 minutes
1 cup (100 g) green beans, washed, tips and strings
   removed, cut diagonally into 1-in (2$\frac{1}{2}$-cm) slices
2 chilies cut diagonally into $\frac{3}{4}$-in (2-cm) slices
1 tablespoon fish sauce
1 tablespoon oyster sauce
1 tablespoon sugar
Freshly ground black pepper to taste
$\frac{1}{2}$ cup Asian basil leaves
$\frac{1}{2}$ cup (125 ml) chicken stock

1 Heat the oil in a wok over high heat until hot. Add the garlic, chilies, and green peppercorns.
2 When the garlic is golden brown and fragrant, add the chicken, baby corn, mushrooms, green beans and red chilies, stirring often for 5 minutes.
3 Add the fish sauce, oyster sauce, sugar, and black pepper to taste. If the dish seems too dry, add chicken stock. Stir to mix well, about 2 minutes. Add basil leaves, remove from heat, and serve with steamed rice.

Serves 4
Preparation time: **10 mins**
Cooking time: **10 mins**

Succulent Turmeric Chicken

1½ lbs (675 g) chicken
  pieces
1½ teaspoons ground
  turmeric
1 teaspoon salt
½ teaspoon freshly
  ground black pepper
⅓ cup (80 ml) oil
2 teaspoons sugar
1 onion, sliced in rings

Serves 4
Preparation time: 30 mins
Cooking time: 25 mins

1 Sprinkle chicken with turmeric, salt, and pepper, mixing to distribute evenly. Set aside for 20 minutes.
2 Heat oil in a wok over high heat. Add the chicken pieces and brown slightly, sealing in the juices, 4 minutes. Reduce heat to medium and fry chicken, stirring frequently, 10 minutes.
3 Add sugar and onion rings and cook, stirring frequently, until onion is lightly browned and chicken cooked, 8 to 10 minutes. Remove with a slotted spatula and drain well on paper towels. Serve hot.

Chicken Chunks with Dried Chilies
(Gung Bao Ji)

If you don't like biting into the whole Sichuan peppercorns, omit them and sprinkle the finished dish with Sichuan Pepper-Salt Powder instead. If sweet thick soy sauce is not available, substitute with 3 tablespoons regular soy sauce mixed with 2 teaspoons sugar.

1 lb (450 g) boneless chicken, cubed
2 tablespoons oil
5 dried red chilies, cut into thirds, seeds shaken out
5 to 8 Sichuan peppercorns
3 cloves garlic, coarsely chopped
6 slices fresh ginger
3 scallions, cut in 1^1/$_2$-in (4-cm) pieces

Marinade
1 tablespoon rice wine
1 teaspoon soy sauce
1 teaspoon sesame oil
^{1}/$_2$ teaspoon sugar
^{1}/$_2$ teaspoon cornstarch dissolved in 4 tablespoons water

Sauce
3 tablespoons soy sauce
1 teaspoon vinegar
1 tablespoon rice wine
1 teaspoon sesame oil
1 teaspoon salt
1 teaspoon cornstarch dissolved in 4 tablespoons water
2 teaspoons sugar

1 Place the chicken chunks in a bowl and cover with the Marinade ingredients. Mix well and set aside for 15 to 20 minutes.
2 Combine the Sauce ingredients and set aside.
3 Heat oil in a wok over high heat until hot, add the dried chilies, and scorch for 30 to 60 seconds. Add the Sichuan peppercorns, garlic and ginger, and stir-fry 30 seconds more.
4 Add the marinated chicken and stir-fry, until chicken changes color and firms, about 4 minutes. Add the sauce, stir to blend all ingredients, cover, reduce heat to medium, and braise for 5 minutes. Remove lid, add scallions, stir to mix with the chicken for 30 seconds, then remove to a serving dish.

Serves 4
Preparation time: **30 mins**
Cooking time: **15 mins**

Spicy Chicken Indian-style

1 green chili
4 cloves garlic
³/₄ in (2 cm) fresh ginger,
  peeled
2 onions, diced
1 tablespoon vinegar or
  lime juice
1 lb (450 g) chicken
  breast, skinned and
  sliced
2 tablespoons oil
1 teaspoon cumin seeds
1 teaspoon fennel seeds
3 tablespoons ground
  cumin
1¹/₄ teaspoons salt
1 tablespoon freshly
  ground black pepper
1 tablespoon lime juice

1 Grind the green chili, garlic, ginger, onion, and vinegar to a paste in a blender or spice grinder. In a large bowl, stir the paste into the chicken and marinate in the refrigerator for at least 1 hour.

2 Heat oil in a wok and stir-fry the cumin and fennel seeds until aromatic. Add the chicken pieces and marinade. Stir in cumin, salt, and ground black pepper, mix well, stirring occasionally until chicken is fairly dry. Sprinkle with lime juice, if desired.

Serves 4
Preparation time: **15 mins**
Cooking time: **20 mins**

Indian Spicy Pork

2 tablespoons oil
1 teaspoon fennel
   seeds, slightly crushed
1 teaspoon cumin seeds
2 onions, diced
2 dried chilies, cut into
   thirds
2 ripe tomatoes, thinly
   sliced
2 cloves garlic, minced
2 green chilies, sliced
2 teaspoons cayenne
   pepper
1 lb (450 g) boneless
   pork, cubed
1 teaspoon salt
1 tablespoon vinegar

1 Heat the oil in a wok and stir-fry the fennel and cumin seeds until aromatic, then add the onions and stir-fry until golden brown, about 10 minutes.
2 Add the chilies, sliced tomatoes, ginger, and garlic, and stir-fry over gentle heat until the oil separates.
3 Add the remaining ingredients except the vinegar. Cook until pork is tender.
4 Just before removing from the heat, add the vinegar, and serve.

Serves 4
Preparation time: **15 mins**
Cooking time: **25 mins**

Stir-fried Fragrant Pork

3 tablespoons oil plus 2 cups (500 ml) for deep-frying
1 onion, diced
3 cloves garlic, minced
2 teaspoons yellow bean paste
2 tablespoons tomato paste
$1/4$ cup (50 g) sugar
$1/4$ cup (60 ml) fish sauce
$1/4$ cup (60 ml) Tamarind Juice (page 7)
Juice from 1 lemon
Rind from 1 lemon
1 cup (160 g) lean pork loin, thinly sliced
1 lb (450 g) rice vermicelli noodles, soaked for 5 minutes and drained
1 cup (40 g) snipped garlic chives or 2 scallions, cut into 1 in ($2^1/2$ cm) lengths
$1/2$ lb (225 g) fresh bean sprouts (optional)
Lemon wedges (optional)

1 Heat 3 tablespoons oil in a wok over medium-high heat. Stir-fry the onion, garlic, yellow bean sauce, and tomato paste until fragrant, about 3 minutes.

2 Add the sugar, fish sauce, and Tamarind Juice, and bring to a boil. Stir in the lemon juice, lemon rind, and pork. Reduce the heat to low and cook uncovered for about 30 minutes, stirring occasionally.

3 Meanwhile, heat 2 cups (500 ml) oil in a large saucepan over medium-high heat. Add the noodles, one handful at a time, to the oil in a single layer. Fry one side until golden and carefully turn the layer of noodles over to fry the other side. Remove the noodles and drain them on paper towels. Repeat until all the noodles are fried.

4 Arrange fried noodles on a serving platter, ladle meat and sauce over them, and garnish with the garlic chives. Surround the noodles with the bean sprouts and garnish with the lemon wedges, if desired. Serve hot.

Serves 4 to 6
Preparation time: **10 mins**
Cooking time: **40 mins**

Red-braised Pork with Orange Peel

You'll find this dish served in almost all Chinese night markets. Home cooks pride themselves on creating their own original blend of seasonings for this dish, which is one of the richest on the entire Chinese menu. Chopped fresh coriander leaves (cilantro) makes an excellent garnish for braised pork shank, because its sharp, fresh taste balances nicely with the rich, sweet flavors of the pork. You may reserve the remaining braising sauce in a jar in the refrigerator and use it as a flavoring sauce for stir-fry cooking, or to braise other foods, such as tofu or fish.

1 whole pork shank, about 3 lb (1 1/2 kg)
1 cup (250 ml) soy sauce
2 cups (500 ml) rice wine
2 cups (500 ml) water
1/2 cup (125 ml) vinegar
1/2 cup sugar (75 g), preferably rock crystal sugar
2 in (5 cm) fresh ginger, sliced
6 scallions, cut into 2-in (5-cm) sections
Peel of one whole fresh orange
1 stick cinnamon, broken into 2 or 3 pieces
1 teaspoon Sichuan peppercorns
2 whole star anise
1/2 lb (225 g) fresh spinach, blanched

1 Fill a large stockpot about two-thirds full of water and bring to a rolling boil. Place the pork shank into the water and bring to a boil, then pour all the water out into the sink, leaving the shank in the pot.

2 Add the remaining ingredients except the spinach to the pot and place pot on high heat and bring the contents to a boil, then reduce heat to medium, cover with lid and simmer for about 3 hours, turning the shank over occasionally. After 2 hours, reduce heat to medium–low, and check from time to time to make sure that the sauce has not evaporated too much. If the level of sauce does not cover at least one-third of the shank, add another cup or two of rice wine mixed in equal portions with water

3 When done, turn off heat, and let pot stand, covered, on stove until ready to serve.

4 To serve, lay a bed of blanched spinach on a platter, then transfer the whole shank onto the spinach. Use a knife and fork to break the shank apart, then drizzle some of the braising sauce over it.

Serves 4
Preparation time: **15 mins**
Cooking time: **3 hours**

116 Healthy Wok and Stir-fry Dishes

Chili-fried Beef

3 to 4 dried chilies,
  cut in thirds, seeds
  removed
2 to 3 fresh red chilies,
  sliced
6 shallots
2 cloves garlic
$1/4$ cup (60 ml) oil
$1^1/4$ lb (600 g) sirloin or
  top round steak, sliced
2 onions, sliced
$3/4$ in (2 cm) fresh
  ginger, minced
1 tablespoon lime juice
2 teaspoons sugar
1 teaspoon salt

Serves 4
Preparation time: **20 mins**
Cooking time: **20 mins**

1 Soak dried chilies in warm water until soft, 10 to 15 minutes. Process soaked chilies, red chilies, shallots and garlic to a smooth paste in a spice grinder or blender, adding a little oil if needed to keep the mixture turning.

2 Heat 2 tablespoons oil in a wok over high heat and stir-fry the beef until lightly browned all over, about 2 minutes. Remove and set aside.

3 Reduce heat to medium, add $1/2$ tablespoon oil, and stir-fry the onion rings until translucent, about 2 minutes. Remove and set aside.

4 Add ginger to wok and stir-fry until golden brown, about 1 minute. Add 2 tablespoons oil to the wok and add chili paste. Stir over low heat until the mixture is fragrant, 5 to 6 minutes. Add salt, sugar, and lime juice.

5 Return the beef, onion and ginger to the wok and add salt, sugar and lime juice. Stir-fry over medium heat until beef is well coated with the chili paste, 1 to 2 minutes. Serve.

Indochine Beef Stew

This dish always wins much praise, and may become your favorite way of serving beef stew. This works well served with rice, pasta, or French bread.

2 stalks lemongrass, finely chopped
1 red or green chili, diced
2 tablespoons fresh ginger, minced
1 teaspoon ground cinnamon
1 teaspoon curry powder
2 tablespoons fish sauce
1 teaspoon salt
$1/4$ teaspoon freshly ground black pepper
2 lbs (1 kg) beef, cut into 1-in ($2^1/_2$-cm) cubes
2 tablespoons oil
1 large onion, peeled and diced
4 cloves garlic
3 cups (750 ml) water
4 tablespoons tomato ketchup
2 star anise
2 carrots, cut in 1-in ($2^1/_2$-cm) chunks
2 potatoes, peeled and cubed into 1-in ($2^1/_2$-cm) chunks
2 daikon, cut in 1-in ($2^1/_2$-cm) chunks (about 2 cups or 250 g)

1 In a large mixing bowl, combine the lemongrass, chili, ginger, cinnamon, curry powder, fish sauce, salt, and black pepper. Add the meat and marinate for 30 minutes.

2 Heat the oil in a large wok over high heat and stir fry the onion and garlic until fragrant, about 2 to 3 minutes.

3 Add the beef and the marinade and stir-fry about 3 minutes or until the beef is browned on all sides. Add the water, tomato paste and star anise. Bring to a boil, then reduce the heat to low and simmer for 1 hour. Add the vegetables and continue simmering until the beef is tender and the vegetables are cooked, about 30 minutes more.

Serves 6–8
Preparation time: **15 mins**
Cooking time: **1 hour**

Beef with Bamboo Shoots

4 tablespoons sesame
  seeds
8 oz (225 g) beef steak,
  thinly sliced
3 tablespoons oil
3 cloves garlic, peeled
  and minced
3 scallions, cut into
  1-in ($2^1/_2$-cm) lengths
8 oz (225 g) bamboo
  shoots, thinly sliced
2 tablespoons fish sauce
1 tablespoon oyster sauce
1 teaspoon salt
$^1/_4$ teaspoon ground
  black pepper

1 Roast the sesame seeds in a clean frying pan or toaster oven for 10 minutes, stirring often to prevent burning. Remove from the heat and crush lightly with a rolling pin to release the flavour.

2 Heat 2 tablespoons oil in a wok over high heat. Stir-fry the beef for about 1 minute. Remove and set aside.

3 Heat the remaining oil in the wok. Add the garlic, scallions, and bamboo shoots. Stir-fry for 3 minutes. Add the fish sauce, oyster sauce, salt, and pepper, stirring until well combined.

4 Return the beef to the wok and add the sesame seeds. Continue to stir-fry for about 3 minutes more. Remove from the heat and serve.

Serves 4–6
Preparation time: **10 mins**
Cooking time: **8 mins**

Sautéed Beef with Chili Sauce and Herbs

$3/_4$ cup (185 ml) thick coconut milk

2 tablespoons Chili Sauce (page 28)

2 lbs (1 kg) beef tenderloin, cut in $1/_2$-in (1-cm) slices

2 oz (60 g) Asian eggplants, sliced

$1^1/_2$ tablespoons green peppercorns

$1^1/_2$ oz (40 g) string beans cut into $1/_2$-in (1-cm) diagonal slices

4 tablespoons Thai fish sauce

3 teaspoons sugar

$1/_3$ cup (90 ml) chicken stock

8 kaffir lime leaves, torn into large pieces

20 Asian basil leaves

6 to 7 chilies, sliced into 1-in ($2^1/_2$-cm) diagonal strips

Serves 4
Preparation time: **20 mins**
Cooking time: **25 mins**

1 Heat the thick coconut milk in a wok or frying-pan. Add the Chili Sauce. Stir continuously until the liquid has reduced by one-third, about 10 minutes.
2 Add the beef and stir for 2 minutes.
3 Add eggplants, peppercorns, and string beans. Stir until cooked. Add fish sauce, sugar, and chicken stock and kaffir lime leaves. Transfer to a serving plate and garnish with basil and red chilies.

Shredded Beef with Bean Sprouts

1 teaspoon rice wine
1 teaspoon light soy
  sauce
1 teaspoon sugar
$^1/_4$ teaspoon pepper
$^1/_4$ cup (60 ml) water
1 teaspoon cornflour
5 oz (150 g) fillet steak,
  shredded
4 tablespoons olive oil
2 shallots, thinly sliced
2 cloves garlic, thinly
  sliced
$2^1/_2$ cups (250 g) bean
  sprouts, tails removed
2 red chilies, seeds
  removed and thinly
  sliced
1 teaspoon sherry
2 tablespoons stock
1 tablespoon oyster
  sauce
1 teaspoon light soy
$^1/_2$ teaspoon sugar
$^1/_4$ teaspoon pepper
1 teaspoon cornflour
  stirred into 1 table-
  spoon water
$^1/_3$ oz (10 g) white leeks
  or chives, cut into 1-in
  (3-cm) sections
1 teaspoon sesame oil

1 Measure the rice wine, light soy sauce, sugar, pepper, water, and cornflour into a medium bowl and stir in the shredded beef. Set aside for 30 minutes to 1 hour, then blend in 2 tablespoons of the oil and continue to marinate for another 15 to 30 minutes.

2 Heat 1 tablespoon of the remaining oil in a wok or frying pan and fry the shredded beef on high heat for 2 minutes or until partially cooked. Set aside.

3 In a clean wok, heat the remaining 1 tablespoon oil; toss in the shallots and garlic and fry until fragrant. Stir-fry the bean sprouts over high heat for about 8 seconds, then pour in the beef and add the chilies. Stir-fry briskly, then sizzle in the wine, add the stock and season with the oyster sauce, soy sauce, sugar, and pepper.

4 Stir the cornflour mixture and add it to the pan. Toss in leeks and sprinkle with the sesame oil. Serve hot.

Serves 2
Preparation time: **15 mins + 45 mins standing**
Cooking time: **10 mins**

Lamb Stir-fried with Piquant Sauce

Instead of scallions you can also use finely sliced onions or mung bean sprouts as a bed for the cooked lamb. If using pork, increase the cooking time to 6 minutes for the pre-cooking, and 6 minutes for the final cooking. This is also an excellent way to prepare venison, wild boar, and other wild game meats.

1 lb (450 g) lamb loin
4 scallions, cut in
　half and into thin strips
3 tablespoons oil

Marinade
1 teaspoon cornstarch
　dissolved in 1 table-
　spoon of water
1 tablespoon soy sauce
1 egg white
$1/2$ teaspoon sugar

Sauce
1 tablespoon yellow
　bean paste or *miso*
1 teaspoon sugar
1 teaspoon salt
2 teaspoons rice wine
1 tablespoon ground
　Sichuan pepper
1 tablespoon sesame oil
1 tablespoon chili sauce
　or chili paste

1 Cut the lamb into thin slices and place in a bowl.
2 To make the Marinade, combine the ingredients, then pour over the lamb and set aside for 15 minutes.
3 Spread the shredded scallions evenly onto a serving plate and set aside.
4 Combine the Sauce ingredients and set aside.
5 Heat 2 tablespoons oil in a wok over high heat until hot. Add the marinated lamb and stir-fry for about 4 minutes. Remove the lamb to a plate and set aside. Discard the oil.
6 Heat remaining 1 tablespoon oil in the wok and when hot, add the Sauce mixture and stir-fry for about 1 minute.
7 Return the lamb to the wok and cook for another 3 to 4 minutes. Remove the lamb and place on top of the shredded scallions on the serving dish.

Serves 4
Preparation time: **15 mins**
Cooking time: **10 mins**

Dry Fried Mutton

4 tablespoons oil
Two 2$^1/_2$-in (2-cm)
  cinnamon sticks
6 cardamom pods
6 cloves
1 teaspoon fennel seeds
1 onion, sliced
2 tomatoes, chopped
1 tablespoon curry
  powder
2 teaspoons *garam
  masala*
1 tablespoon ground
  coriander powder
500 ml (2 cups) water
1 lb (450 g) mutton,
  cubed
1 teaspoon salt

Spice Paste
2 onions, finely sliced
1 tablespoon ginger
1 large clove garlic
1 teaspoon black
  peppercorns
2 sprigs curry leaves,
  remove central stalk
3 dried chilies, cut into
  $^1/_2$-in (1-cm) lengths
$^1/_3$ cup (20 g) mint
  leaves
$^1/_3$ cup (20 g) fresh
  coriander leaves,
  chopped

1 Grind the Spice Paste ingredients until fine. Set aside.
2 Heat the oil and fry the cinnamon, cardamoms, cloves, and fennel until aromatic. Add the onion and tomatoes and sauté until the onion turns golden brown, about 3 minutes.
3 Stir in the ground spice paste, the meat curry powder, *garam masala*, and coriander powder.
4 Add the water and mutton. Cook until the mutton is tender and the liquid evaporates, about 30 minutes. Season with salt to taste.

Serves 4
Preparation time: **40 mins**
Cooking time: **33 mins**

Complete Recipe Listing

Beef with Bamboo Shoots 120

Bengali Fish Curry 78

Black Hokkien Noodles 56

Broccoli Stir-fried with Ginger and Onion 13

Brown Rice with Mixed Vegetables 60

Carrots and Shiitake Mushrooms Stir-fried with Ginger 8

Carrots Stir-fried with Coconut and Curry Spices 10

Chicken Chunks with Dried Chilies 108

Chicken with Coriander Yogurt Gravy 102

Chili-fried Beef 116

Chinese Cabbage and Tofu Skin Stir-fried with Ginger 18

Classic Chicken, Pork, or Beef Thai Fried Rice 68

Crabs in Garlic and Pepper Sauce 89

Diced Vegetables Stir-fried with Ginger and Sichuan Pepper 26

Dry Fried Mutton 126

Eggplant with Fragrant Meat Sauce 32

Fish Stir-fried with Black Beans and Pepper 72

Five-spice Chicken with Garlic and Scallions 98

Fragrant Shrimp Fried Rice 64

Gung Bao Squid with Dried Chilies 96

Home-style "Leftovers" Fried Rice 66

Hot and Spicy Tofu 40

Indian Fried Rice 70

Indian Spicy Pork 111

Indochine Beef Stew 118

Lamb Stir-fried with Piquant Sauce 124

Malaysian-style Fried Egg Noodles 54

Red-braised Pork with Orange Peel 114

Rice Noodles with Chicken and Chinese Broccoli 48

Sautéed Beef with Chili Sauce and Herbs 121

Sautéed Chinese Peashoots with Garlic and Sichuan Pepper 25

Savory Seared Runner Beans 24

Seafood and Vegetable Stir-fry 92

Seafood Fried Rice in Pineapple 62

Shredded Beef with Bean Sprouts 122

Shrimp Masala 84

Shrimp Curry 86

Sichuan Shrimps with Chili Sauce 80

Snow Peas and Shiitake Mushrooms Stir-fried with Ginger and Scallions 20

Spicy Chicken Indian-style 110

Spicy Spinach Stir-fried with Tofu Skin 42

Spicy Stir-fried Rice Vermicelli 46

Spicy Stir-fried Sichuan Squid 94

Spinach Stir-fried with Garlic 12

Stir-fried Bean Thread Noodles 58

Stir-fried Chicken with Asian Basil and Vegetables 104

Stir-fried Cumin Chicken 100

Stir-fried Eggplant with Pungent Chili Sauce 28

Stir-fried Fragrant Pork 112

Stir-fried Green Beans with Bean Sprouts and Fresh Chilies 22

Stir-fried Mustard Leaves and Lentils 16

Stir-fried Rice Sticks with Beef in Soy Gravy 52

Stir-fried Shredded Potatoes 34

Stir-fried Sliced Fish with Ginger 76

Stir-fried Thai Noodles with Shrimps 50

Succulent Turmeric Chicken 106

Sweet and Sour Eggplant 30

Tangy Tamarind Shrimps 82

Tempe and Tofu Stir-fry 45

Thai Mussels with Lemongrass 90

Tofu, Green Beans, and Peanuts Stir-fried with Chili and Garlic 38

Tomatoes Stir-fried with Onions and Pine Nuts 36

Vietnamese Caramel Fish 74

Vietnamese-style Spicy Shrimps 88

Water Spinach Stir-fried with Fermented Black Beans 14